Gregor Chant

FOR CHURCH AND SCHOOL

BY

SISTER MARY ANTONINE GOODCHILD, O.P.

DIRECTOR

OF THE DEPARTMENT OF MUSIC EDUCATION

ROSARY COLLEGE

RIVER FOREST, ILLINOIS

GINN AND COMPANY

BOSTON · NEW YORK · CHICAGO · ATLANTA · DALLAS · COLUMBUS
SAN FRANCISCO · TORONTO · LONDON

COPYRIGHT, 1944, BY GINN AND COMPANY

345.9

Messrs. Desclée & Cie. have, as an exception, authorized the firm of GINN AND COMPANY *to use, in the book* GREGORIAN CHANT FOR CHURCH AND SCHOOL, *the rhythmic signs and the melodies taken from the Solesmes editions, which are their exclusive property.*

The Athenæum Press
GINN AND COMPANY · PRO-
PRIETORS · BOSTON · U.S.A.

Nihil Obstat
JOSEPH T. KUSH, S.T.B., C.G.M.
CENSOR DEPUTATUS

Imprimatur
✢ SAMUEL A. STRITCH
ARCHBISHOP OF CHICAGO

CHICAGO, APRIL 17, 1944

Museo San Marco, Florence

ANNUNCIATION (DETAIL) BY FRA ANGELICO

To Mary

OUR HEAVENLY MOTHER AND MEDIATRIX

I DEDICATE THIS LITTLE VOLUME.

Foreword

THE AIM of this little volume is primarily to fulfill a definite need, namely: to supply suitable Plain-Chant material for adolescent youth; to present the material in a manner wholly understandable, and therefore interesting to pupils of this grade level; to include nothing which might render the book less appropriate for use in church than in school; and lastly, but of greatest importance, to create a true love for and an appreciation of the official music of the Church.

I wish to express grateful appreciation for assistance and encouragement to

His Eminence, LUIGI CARDINAL MAGLIONE, Secretary of State to His Holiness, Vatican City, Italy;

His Eminence, EUGENE CARDINAL TISSERANT, Secretary, Sacred Congregation for the Oriental Church, Vatican City, Italy;

The Most Reverend AMLETO GIOVANNI CICOGNANI, D.D., Apostolic Delegate to the United States of America;

The Most Reverend SAMUEL ALPHONSUS STRITCH, D.D., Archbishop of Chicago;

The Very Reverend Monsignor DANIEL F. CUNNINGHAM, LL.D., Superintendent of Schools, Archdiocese of Chicago;

The Very Reverend Monsignor REYNOLD HILLENBRAND, S.T.D., Rector, Saint Mary of the Lake Seminary, Mundelein, Illinois;

The Very Reverend T. S. McDERMOTT, O.P., S.T.Lr., LL.D., Provincial, Province of Saint Joseph;

DOM ERMIN VITRY, O.S.B., Editor of Caecilia and Director of Liturgical Music, Saint Mary's Institute, O'Fallon, Missouri;

The Reverend JOHN DE DEO OLDEGEERING, O.F.M., Director of Music, Junior Seminary, Cincinnati, Ohio;

The Reverend EDWIN V. HOOVER, Mus. D., former Director of Music, Quigley Preparatory Seminary, Chicago, Illinois;

FOREWORD

The Reverend JOSEPH T. KUSH, C.G.M., Music Director, Saint Mary of the Lake Seminary, Mundelein, Illinois;

Sister MARY AQUINAS DEVLIN, O.P., Ph.D., Head of the Department of English, Rosary College, River Forest, Illinois;

Sister MARY REPARATA MURRAY, O.P., B.L.S., Director, Rosary College Library School, River Forest, Illinois;

Sister WINIFRED MARY CARMODY, O.P., Ph.D., Head of the Department of Classical Languages, Rosary College, River Forest, Illinois;

Mademoiselle MARGUERITE-MARIE VUILLEMIN, Vatican City, Italy; at present, Cataloguer, Catholic University of America Library.

SR. M.A.

Contents

i
	PAGE
THE STORY OF GREGORIAN CHANT	3

ii
THEORETICAL INTRODUCTION TO THE CHANT . . . 6

The Staff and Notation: The Staff, 6 · Clefs, 6 · Notation, 7 · Origin of Syllables, 8 · *Hymn to St. John the Baptist*, 8 · Modes, 9 · Gregorian Scales, 9 · Tonics, 9 · Finals, 9 · Dominants, 9 · Rhythm, 10 · Ictus, 10 · The Singing of the Chant, 11 · Breathing, 11 · Guide, 12 · Kinds of Chant: Syllabic, 12 · Neumatic, 12 · Melismatic, 12

iii
READY REFERENCE 14

Ecclesiastical Pronunciation of the Latin: Vowels, 14 · Diphthongs, 14 Consonants, 14 · Neums, 15 · Neums of Two Notes: Clivis, 15 · Podatus, 15 Neums of Three or More Notes: Torculus, 16 · Porrectus, 16 · Scandicus, 16 Salicus, 16 · Climacus, 16 · The Extension of Neums, 16 · Neums of Four Notes: Scandicus Flexus, 17 · Salicus Flexus, 17 · Porrectus Flexus, 17 Climacus Resupinus, 17 · Torculus Resupinus, 17 · Pes Subpunctis, 18 Pes Subpunctis Resupinus, 18 · Scandicus Subpunctis, 18 · Torculus Resupinus, 18 · Torculus Resupinus Flexus, 18 · Porrectus Flexus, 19 Porrectus Flexus Resupinus, 19 · Liquescent Neums: Liquescent Clivis, 19 Liquescent Podatus, 19 · Liquescent Torculus, 19 · Episema, 19 · Quilisma, 20 · Pressus, 20 · Bistropha, 20 · Tristropha, 20

iv
PRESENTATION OF THE MODES AND THEIR TRANSPOSITION . 21

Modes, 21 · Clefs, 22 · Aids to Mode I, 22 · Sequence, 22 · *Victimae Paschali*, 23 · Aids to Mode II, 25 · *Tantum Ergo*, 25 · Mode II, Transcribed into Modern Notation, 26 · Aids to Mode III, 26 · *Tantum Ergo*, 26 · Mode IV: *Gloria Patri*, 27 · Mode V: *Tantum Ergo*, 28 · Aids to Mode VI, 28 · *Ave Verum*, 29 · Accidental, 29 · Mode VII: *Panis Angelicus*, 30 · Mode VIII: *Pacificus*, 31 · Transposition of the Modes, 31 · *O Filii*, 32

v
REPERTORY 34

A List of Selections in this Chapter, 34

Gregorian Chant

FOR CHURCH AND SCHOOL

THE STORY OF GREGORIAN CHANT

THE EARLY CHRISTIANS had to worship God in secret much of the time, but we are told that they sang during their assemblies, undoubtedly the psalms which the Jews among them had been accustomed to sing or chant in the synagogue before their conversion. These chants, therefore, needed to be remodeled according to Christian ideals and principles; and so as soon as the persecution of the Christians had ceased (fourth century), the bishops of the Church ordered the necessary changes to be made.

Saint Ambrose, bishop of Milan, was foremost in this reform. The chant which was established and approved during his time bears the name "Ambrosian Chant." It was simple and beautiful, and the Milanese, to honor the memory of their sainted bishop, still use this chant, whether or not in its original form we do not know.

We may well suppose that many changes were made in the chant, and that new chants were written during the period from the time of Saint Ambrose to the pontificate of Gregory I (590–604). This sainted Pope was called by historians Gregory the Great, and justly so, for he was not only the greatest man of his age, but his works have influenced all succeeding ages. He is credited with a certain final arrangement of the chant, which, some two hundred years later, received the name "Gregorian Chant."

Pope Gregory's earnest desire was to have the chant sung as perfectly as possible, and for this end he established a Song School called the *Schola Cantorum* (skō′-lä kän-tō′-ro͝om), in which choir singers and teachers of singing received thorough training in the chant. These teachers were then sent to various places, where they in turn trained other choirs, and thus knowledge of the chant was spread into the newly converted countries, and transmitted from generation to generation.

We read that the Emperor Charlemagne, two hundred years after Pope Gregory's time, became so enthusiastic upon hearing the chant that he ordered it sung throughout his empire, and even took members of his own chapel choir to Rome so that they might be properly trained in the Schola Cantorum.

And thus Gregorian chant flourished until a new style of music called diaphony (dē-ăf′-ō-ny), which means two sounds heard together, was introduced. In this music a second part was added to the original Gregorian melodies, forming a harmony which you would today find very crude and uninteresting. This type of music led to polyphony (pō-lĭf′-ō-ny), which means the combination of many voice parts, melody against melody. Some of you have sung selections from Palestrina's polyphonic music, and I am sure you found it very beautiful, but it is not so well suited to the liturgy of the Church as is the Gregorian Chant.

The chant continued to be sung for several centuries after polyphonic music came into existence, but its rendition became worse and worse because the people preferred to sing in parts, and because of the many abuses that were being introduced into Church music. As a result the chant gradually declined, and in time its beautiful free rhythm was forgotten, and its general use was cast aside to make way for a style of music that is anything but devotional.

Many unsuccessful attempts were made to restore the chant. It was not until 1903, however, when Pope Pius X wrote to the entire Christian world a letter [1] in which he asked for a reform in Church music, that lay people began seriously to study Gregorian Chant.

The more one understands this music, the more one loves it and the more one realizes how much more devotional it is than any other style of music. It is truly beautiful and belongs to the Church. We should therefore consider it a privilege and a duty

---

[1] This letter was called *Motu Proprio* (mō′-tōō prō′-prē-ō) meaning of his own accord, that is, not on the advice of others, but for reasons which the pope himself deemed sufficient. — Catholic Encyclopedia, Vol. X.

to learn all we possibly can about the chant, and count ourselves fortunate if this opportunity is given us.

QUESTIONS

1. What did the early Christians sing in their assemblies?

2. When were these chants changed to conform to Christian ideals?

3. Who was foremost in this reform?

4. Who brought about the final arrangement of the chant?

5. What has the chant ever since been called?

6. What was the *Schola Cantorum*?

7. How did Charlemagne promote the use of the chant?

8. What change in the style of music took place in the ninth century?

9. What was the effect of this change upon Church music?

10. Who asked for a reform in Church music?

ii

THEORETICAL INTRODUCTION TO THE CHANT

THE STAFF AND NOTATION

The Staff. At the time when Gregorian Chant was at its height, — we might call it the "golden age" of Gregorian Chant, — there was not the means that we have of recording music. The staff and notation did not come into existence until the eleventh century, and so there was no way of showing the exact melody one was to sing. Choirmasters used symbols, which looked something like our shorthand. These were called neums, and were written above the words, simply to help the choirmaster to remember whether the melody went up or down, or whether the distance from one tone to the next was close or far removed. This meant, of course, that the chant had to be taught by rote, that is, the pupils singing what the choirmaster had sung to them. In the first half of the eleventh century, Guido (gwē'-dō), a Benedictine monk of Arezzo (ă-rĕt'-sō) in Tuscany, Italy, perfected a four-line staff, upon which ever since that time Gregorian music has been written.

Clefs. In order that the singers might know just what pitch to sing, the staff alone was not sufficient; a key was necessary, so two clefs were provided, a *Do* clef

and a *Fa* clef

The *Do* clef may be placed on any except the first line, but the

Fa clef is usually on the third line. The lines and spaces of the Gregorian staff have not definite letter names such as have been given to the lines and spaces of the modern five-line staff, so that *Do* may be *C*, or it may be any other pitch that will bring the chant melody within an easy singing range.

Notation. Modern music is written in round notes, differing in time values, such as

The whole note	𝅝
The half note	𝅗𝅥
The quarter note	♩
The eighth note	♪
The sixteenth note	𝅘𝅥𝅯

Gregorian music is written in various shaped notes all equal in time value, regardless of shape, such as

The *punctum* (pŏŏnk′-tŏŏm)	■
The *virga* (vĭr′-gah)	ᛈ
The *rhombus* (rŏm′-bŏŏs)	♦
The *quilisma* (kwē-lĭs′-mah)	ᴡ
The *liquescent* (lĭ-kwĕs′-ent) *note*	↲

The *punctum*, however, is the only note which may be used alone.

SYLLABLES

Guido, knowing that since music is a language, the ability to read it would afford far more pleasure and enjoyment than mere rote singing, was anxious to provide some means whereby this ability might be more easily acquired. One day, upon his newly completed staff, Guido wrote the melody of the following hymn to Saint John the Baptist, and as each succeeding line of the hymn, with the exception of the last, started one degree higher than the preceding one, a new idea occurred to him. He took the first syllable from the first word of each line and applied these to the tones of the scale, thus:

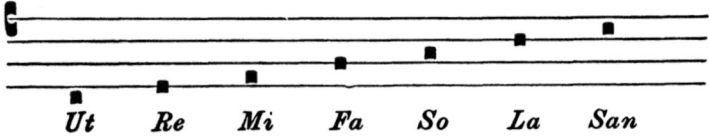

These are the syllables which are in general use today, with the exception of *Ut* and *San*, which have been changed to *Do* and *Ti*. By means of these syllables one can more easily learn to read music.

Hymn to St. John the Baptist

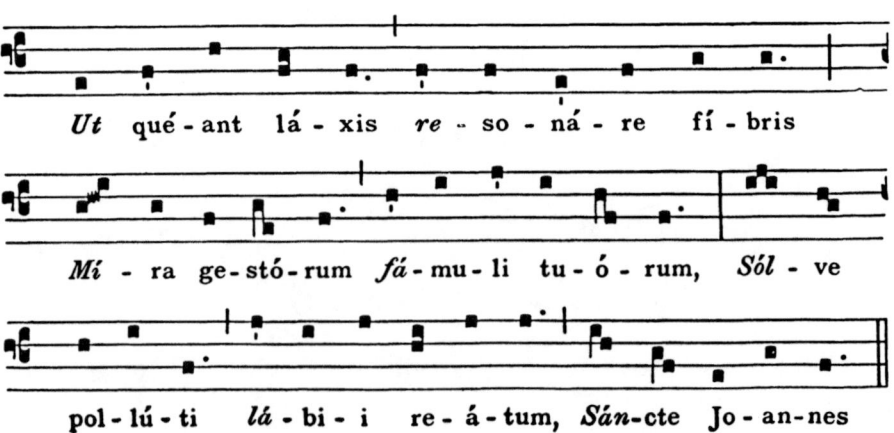

> That thy servants may
>   with full voices
>   sing the marvels of
>   thy deeds
> remove from us the reproach
>   of sin-polluted lip,
> O holy John.

MODES

In modern music there are only two modes,[1] the major and the minor mode. In the major mode there are fifteen scales, each of which has a different *tonic*, or *key tone*, but as far as the pattern is concerned they are all alike, each scale consisting of two whole tones, a half tone, three whole tones and a half tone. The half tones always occur between *Mi-Fa*, and *Ti-Do*.

In Gregorian music there are eight modes, but we shall think of them as eight scales, for the terms *mode* and *scale*, as regards the chant, are identical. In each succeeding Gregorian scale, the half tones occur between different steps.

Tonics. The syllabic (sĭ-lăb'-ĭk), or syllable name for the *tonic*, or tone upon which every major scale is built, is *Do*. In Gregorian music there are only four *tonics*, *Re, Mi, Fa, So*; but these are called *finals*, because the melody always ends on one of these tones, according to the mode it is in, unless the melody is too high and has to be transposed. (Transposition will be explained when the problem is met.)

Dominants. The tone of greatest importance, after the tonic, is the dominant. In modern music the dominant is always five tones above the tonic. This rule applies to some of the Gregorian modes, but not to all of them. It will be best, therefore, to explain what tone is the dominant of each mode as the mode is studied. This tone exerts a powerful influence over the entire mode.

---

[1] Mode, in music, refers to the different arrangement of tones.

RHYTHM

Rhythm is the very life of music. It is rhythm that unites, organizes, and arranges the different musical sounds into perfect order, and the more perfect the order, the better is the music. Saint Augustine called rhythm " the art of beautiful movement," and this art is strikingly illustrated in the chant, for while the rhythm is free from the restrictions of mathematical measurement, it is alive with beautifully ordered movement.

In measured music, where the rhythm is said to be fixed, each measure must be uniformly maintained throughout the composition, which implies a regular recurrence of accent, but where the rhythm is free, the melody moves in groups of two and three tones, which groups alternate freely with each other.

Ictus. This grouping of notes is determined by what is called an *ictus*. The ictus is indicated by a short vertical line underneath the note which corresponds to the first note of the measure in modern music.

In modern music this note would be accented, whereas in Gregorian music the ictus does not necessarily mean a strong, but merely a slight, emphasis. Accent in the chant refers mostly to the words. Every Latin word of two or more syllables has what is called a *tonic* accent on the principal syllable, such as *Cré-do in ú-num Dé-um*. The ictus and the word accent may or may not occur at the same place.

Latin words of two syllables are always accented on the first syllable, thus: *Dé-us, mé-us, ú-nus*, and the like. In words of more than two syllables the tonic accent will occur on the first or second syllable from the last (the accents come at intervals of two or three syllables). A word that consists of more than three syllables must have one or more secondary accents. Example: *Ju-stí-fi-cá-ti-ó-ni-bus*.

THE SINGING OF THE CHANT

To be beautiful the chant must be beautifully sung. The voices should be kept light. That does not mean suppressed or lifeless, but clear and mellow. There must be no harsh or forced tones, or all beauty disappears. The chant must not be sung too rapidly, but neither should it be sung too slowly.

Breath Marks. You have heard a great deal about the correct phrasing of songs. This is partly accomplished by the proper breath control. In the chant there are signs which show just where a breath may be taken without interrupting the phrase. These are here shown and explained.

1. The short vertical bar through the fourth line of the staff allows one to take a quick breath, if necessary.

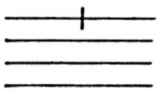

2. The bar crossing the second and third lines of the staff marks off a member, or portion, of a phrase, and is usually preceded by a longer note, which allows a pause of about one beat in length.

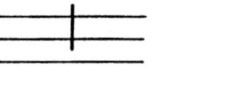

3. The full bar marks off a phrase, and as this also is preceded by a longer note, there may be a slightly longer pause.

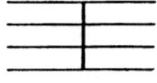

4. The double bar indicates the end of a section, and permits a good deep breath.

We may compare these breath marks to the punctuation in language. Both are intended to give more expressive meaning to the content. You know how necessary punctuation marks are, and how uninteresting and meaningless the printed page would be without them. Proper breathing is just as important. You already know that to take a breath in the middle of a word or phrase is wrong. Be careful, therefore, to breathe at the right place in the chant, and at no other place.

Guide. At the end of each line there will be a small note to indicate the pitch of the first note of the next line.

KINDS OF CHANT

Syllabic (sĭ-lăb′-ĭk). A chant in which there is only one note to a syllable, or where only a very few neums appear.

Neumatic (noō-mă′-tĭk). A chant in which neums are frequently employed.

Melismatic (mĕl-ĭz-mă′-tĭk). A chant in which there are many notes to one word or to one syllable.

QUESTIONS

1. When was the four-line staff perfected and by whom?
2. How was the chant taught before that time?
3. How many clefs are there in Gregorian music?
4. Name the clefs and tell where each may be used.
5. How does Gregorian notation differ from modern notation in so far as shape and time values are concerned?
6. What is the origin of the syllables which are in general use today?
7. What changes have been made in these syllables since they were first introduced?

THEORETICAL INTRODUCTION TO THE CHANT

8. How many modes are there in modern music? What are these modes called?

9. How many modes are there in Gregorian music?

10. What is meant by a *final*?

11. What tone is next in importance after the *tonic*?

12. How do modern and Gregorian music differ as to rhythm?

13. What do you understand by the term *ictus*?

14. Does the accent in the chant apply mostly to the music or to the words?

15. What is meant by *tonic accent*?

16. Where does the tonic accent fall?

17. How should the chant be sung?

18. Explain the different kinds of breath marks.

19. What is the *guide*? What is its purpose?

iii

READY REFERENCE

ECCLESIASTICAL PRONUNCIATION OF THE LATIN

Vowels

    a is sounded like *a* in "father"
    ē is sounded like *a* in "fame"
    ĕ is sounded like *e* in "met"
    i and **y** are sounded like *ee* in "meet"
    o is sounded like *o* in "no"
    u is sounded like *oo* in "boot"

Diphthongs

ae, oe, are sounded like *ay* in "day," except when two dots are placed above the **ë**, in which case each vowel is given a distinct sound.

au is sounded like *ou* in "house."

eu though forming one syllable is sounded *ā'oo*.

As a general rule each vowel is sounded separately, even though the vowel is doubled as in *filii*, which is pronounced fee-lee-ee.

Consonants

Those consonants which differ in sound from their usage in the English language are **c, cc, sc, ch, g, gn,** and **ti.**

c before **e, ae, oe, i, y** receives the sound of *ch* as in "chair." Example: *dul'-ce* (dul'-chā), *cae'-lum* (chā'-lŏom).

c before **a, o, u, au** receives the sound of *k* as in "kite."

cc before **e, ae, oe, i, y** receives the sound *tch*. Example: *ecce* (et'-chāy).

sc before **e, ae, oe, i, y** receives the sound of *sh*. Example: *de-scen-dit* (dā-shen'-deet).

ch before any vowel receives the sound of *k*, as in *brachium* (brah'-kē-oom).

g before **e, ae, oe, i, y** receives the soft sound as in the words *An'-ge-lus, re-gi'-na*. In every other case **g** is hard, as in *gladius*, unless followed by **n**.

gn receives the sound of *ni* in *union*. Example: *agnus* (ah'-nyoos).

h receives the sound of *k* in *mihi* (mē-ke) and *nihil* (nee'-keel). In all other cases it is not sounded.

j is sounded like the English *y* in *yes*. Example: *je'-su* (yā'-soo). The **i** in *alleluia* is sounded the same (al-le-loo'-ya).

s is always sounded like *s* in *yes*.

ti when followed by a vowel and preceded by any letter except *s, t, x,* is sounded like *tsee*. Example: *gratias* (gra'-tsee-as).

x before **c** is sounded like *gg* and the **c** like *sh*. Example: *excelsis* (egg-shĕl'-sees).

A consonant between two vowels belongs to the vowel following it. Example: *bo'-nae, ti'-bi*, etc.

NEUMS

A combination of two or more notes is called a neum.

There should be no drill on the following neums, or any attempt at memorizing them, except as they occur in the chants. Frequent reference to these pages and a little written work will soon familiarize you with the various neums, so that reading the chant from Gregorian notation will afford no more difficulty than reading from modern notation.

Neums of Two Notes

Clivis (klē'-vĭs)

Podatus (pō-dah'-to͝os)

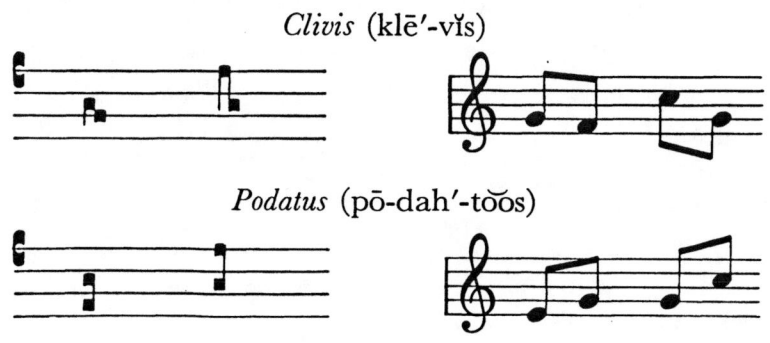

Neums of Three or more Notes

The Extension of Neums. A *scandicus* and a *climacus* may be extended without change of name, provided the notes continue in the same direction.

NOTE. In a *scandicus* the three notes are close together and the *ictus* falls on the first note. In the *salicus* the *punctum* is slightly separated from the *podatus* and the *ictus* falls on the second note.

A *neum* may also be extended by the addition of a *punctum* close to the first or last note, thus:

Neums of Four Notes. When a descending note is added to an ascending group, the term *Flexus* is applied.

Scandicus Flexus (flĕx′-sōos)

Salicus Flexus

Porrectus Flexus

When an ascending note is added to a descending group, the term *Resupinus* is applied.

Climacus Resupinus (rā-sōo-pē′-nŏos)

Torculus Resupinus

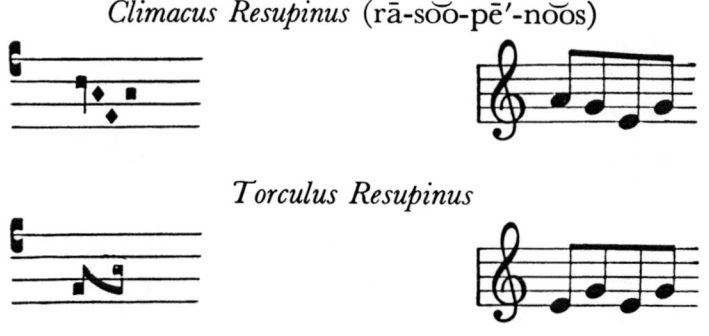

A *pes*, or *podatus* as it is now called, and a *scandicus* may further be enlarged as follows:

Pes Subpunctis (soŏb-poŏnk′-tĭs)

Pes Subpunctis Resupinus

Scandicus Subpunctis

A *torculus* may further be enlarged by bending downward again after the ascent.

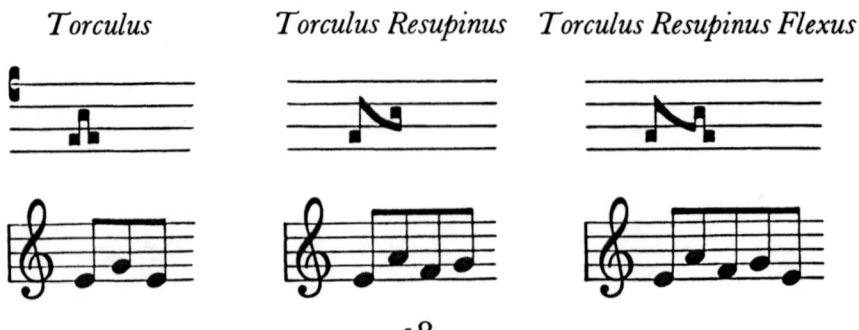

Torculus   Torculus Resupinus   Torculus Resupinus Flexus

READY REFERENCE

A *porrectus* may further be enlarged by turning back after having descended.

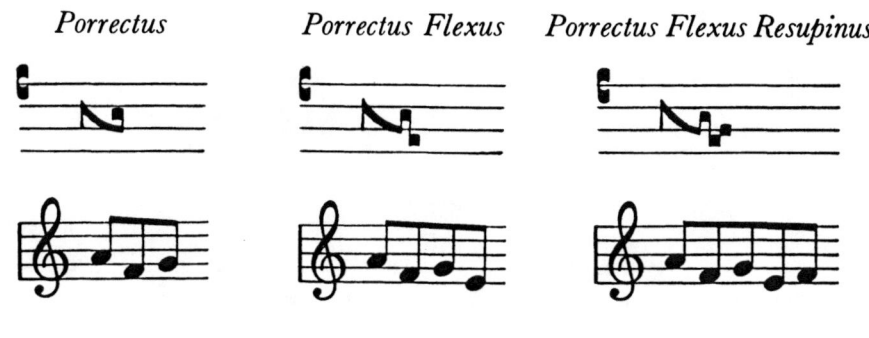

Liquescent Neums

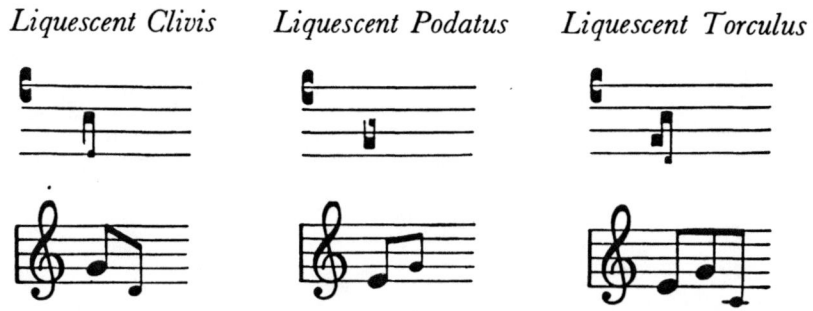

A *liquescent* may appear as the last note of a group, or even as the last two notes. The shape of the note does not affect the time value.

Episema. This is a horizontal line over a single note, over one of a group of notes, or over an entire group. It means a slight prolongation of these notes, but not the doubling of them. (This line is often under the note instead of above it.)

Quilisma (kwē-lĭs'-mah). This is an indented note appearing only in ascending groups. The note before the *quilisma* is slightly prolonged, and the *quilisma* is sung very softly. Time values remain the same.

Pressus (prĕs'-sōōs). A *pressus* is formed by the meeting of two *neums* on the same degree of the staff, or by a single *punctum* meeting a *neum* of the same degree of the staff.

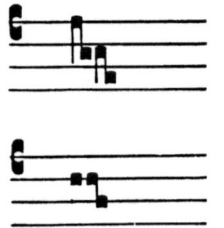   

The *ictus* always falls on the first note of the *pressus*.

Bistropha (bĭs'-trō-fah). Two notes on the same degree of the staff.

Tristropha (trĭs'-trō-fah). Three notes on the same degree of the staff.

iv

PRESENTATION OF THE MODES

MODES

IN MODERN MUSIC the scales are divided into *major* and *minor* modes. In Gregorian music the scales are divided into *authentic* and *plagal* modes. Just as each *major* scale has a relative *minor*, so each *authentic* scale has a relative *plagal*. The relative minor is found a minor third (three half steps) below the major. It has the same signature as the major, and *do* remains the same in both modes. The related *plagal* is found four degrees [1] below the *authentic*, and the *final* is the same in both modes.

The *major* scale extends from *do* to *do*; the minor scale from *la* to *la*. Example:

    1   2   3   4   5   6   7   8 = *Major scale.*
                        6   7   8   2   3   4   5   6 = *Minor scale.*

In Gregorian music the extent of each scale is as follows:

MODE I				<u>2</u>	3	4	5	⑥	7	8	2	. . . . Authentic
MODE II	6	7	1	<u>2</u>	3	④	5	6				. . . . Plagal
MODE III				<u>3</u>	4	5	6	7	⑧	2	3	. . . . Authentic
MODE IV	7	1	2	<u>3</u>	4	5	⑥	7				. . . . Plagal
MODE V				<u>4</u>	5	6	7	⑧	2	3	4	. . . . Authentic
MODE VI	1	2	3	<u>4</u>	5	⑥	7	8				. . . . Plagal
MODE VII				<u>5</u>	6	7	8	②	3	4	5	. . . . Authentic
MODE VIII	2	3	4	<u>5</u>	6	7	⑧	2				. . . . Plagal

It will be observed that *Modes* I, III, V, VII, are *authentic modes*, and that *Modes* II, IV, VI, VIII, are *plagal modes*. The *dominant* of each *authentic* mode is a fifth above the *final*, except in *Mode* III. In this mode the dominant would, according to the rule, fall upon *Ti*, but since that tone is often flatted, and therefore not always the same, the dominant has been moved up to *Do*. The *dominant* of each *plagal* mode is a third below that of its related *authentic mode*, except in *Mode* VIII, where it moves up a tone for the same reason as stated above. (The finals are underlined; the dominants are encircled.)

[1] Each line and space of the staff is considered a degree.

CLEFS

The *Do* clef is on the fourth line in *Modes* I, III, IV, VI, VIII, and on the third line in *Modes* V and VII, unless the chant is transposed. The *Fa* clef is on the third line in *Mode* II unless the chant is transposed. The modes are always indicated by either a Roman or an Arabic numeral in the left-hand margin.

AIDS TO MODE I

The chant, "Victimae Paschali," here presented, is in the first mode, as indicated by the figure I in the left-hand margin. The final is *Re*; the dominant is *La*. The *Do* clef is on the fourth line, as it always is in the first mode, unless the chant is transposed.

1. This chant is syllabic. Why?
2. Can you name the neums which appear in this chant?

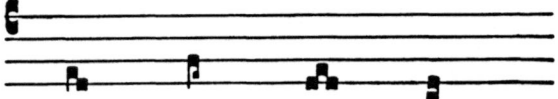

3. Locate an episema. What does it mean?
4. What is the significance of a dot after a note?
5. If *Do* were on the fourth line in any of the songs which you are accustomed to sing, what would be the key? Just consider that you are singing in that key and you will have no difficulty in reading the chant.

"Victimae Paschali" is the Sequence for Easter. It was written about the middle of the eleventh century.

The word *sequence* comes from the Latin word *sequi*, meaning "to follow." Formerly the final *a* of the *Alleluia* was sung to a long melody, and since this followed the *Alleluia*, it was called a *Sequence*. In the eighth century the custom arose of setting words to this melody. Finally the entire hymn was called a *Sequence*.

There are today five Sequences in use:

Victimae Paschali, for Easter
Lauda Sion, for Corpus Christi
Veni Sancte Spiritus, for Pentecost
Stabat Mater, for Seven Dolors of B. V. M.
Dies Irae, for Requiem Masses

Whenever a hymn appears that is not familiar to you, there will be an English translation of it.

To the Paschal Victim, Christians, bring your sacrifice of praise.
The Lamb hath redeemed the sheep.
The innocent Christ hath reconciled sinners to the Father.
Death and Life have fought in a strange conflict;
The Prince of Life, Who died, now reigns living.
Tell us, Mary, what didst thou see on the way?
" I saw the tomb of the living Christ and the glory of the risen Christ.
I saw the Angels, His witnesses, the napkin and the linen cloths.
Christ, my hope, hath risen. He will go before you into Galilee."
We know that Christ hath truly risen from the dead.
Victorious King, have mercy on us. Amen. Alleluia.

Victimae Paschali

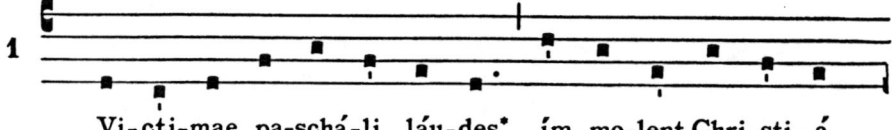

Vi-cti-mae pa-schá-li láu-des* ím-mo-lent Chri-sti-á-

ni. A-gnus red-é-mit ó-ves: Chri-stus ín-no-cens Pa-tri

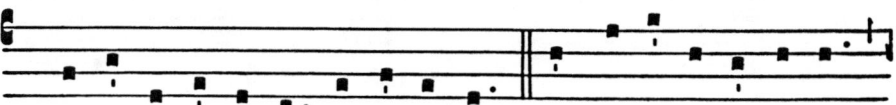

re-con-ci-li-á-vit pec-ca-tó-res. Mors et vi-ta du-él-lo

NOTE. A dot after the note doubles its value.

PRESENTATION OF THE MODES

AIDS TO MODE II

1. What clef is used?

2. This clef marks the place of what syllable?

3. From that syllable find *Do*, and then read the chant as you would modern music.

4. Two neums, which are new to you, appear in this chant. Refer to pages 16 and 18.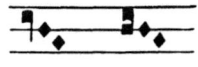

Tantum Ergo

1. Tan-tum er-go Sa-cra-mén-tum Ve-ne-ré-mur cér-
2. Ge-ni-tó-ri Ge-ni-tó-que Laus et ju-bi-lá-

nu-i: Et an-tí-quum do-cu-mén-tum Nó-vo cé-dat
ti-o: Sá-lus, hó-nor, vír-tus quo-que Sit et be-ne-

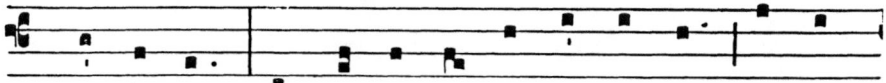

rí-tu-i: Prae-stet fí-des sup-ple-mén-tum Sén-su-
dí-cti-o: Pro-ce-dén-ti ab u-tró-que Cóm-par-

um de-fé-ctu-i.
sit lau-dá-ti-o. A-men.

℣.[1] Pánem de cáelo praestitísti eis. (Alleluia.)
℟.[2] Omne delectaméntum in se habéntem. (Alleluia.)
(Prayer) ℟. Amen.

[1] ℣. is a sign which stands for the word *versicle*. A versicle is a short sentence sung by the priest and followed by a response from the choir or congregation.
[2] R. or ℟. stands for the word *response*.

GREGORIAN CHANT FOR CHURCH AND SCHOOL

For the English translation of the hymn presented above refer to the last two stanzas of the "Pange Lingua," p. 114.

Mode II, Transcribed into Modern Notation

AIDS TO MODE III

1. What is the final in this chant?
2. What is the dominant?
3. How many times does the dominant appear?
4. Does the chant (excluding the *Amen*) end on the final?

Tantum Ergo

1. Tan-tum er-go Sa-cra-mén-tum Ve-ne-ré-mur cér-nu-i:
2. Ge-ni-tó-ri, Ge-ni-tó-que Laus et ju-bi-lá-ti-o:

Et an-tí-quum do-cu-mén-tum No-vo cé-dat rí-tu-i:
Sá-lus, hó-nor, vír-tus quo-que Sit et be-ne-di-cti-o:

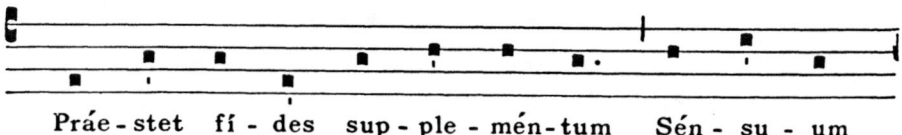

Práe-stet fí-des sup-ple-mén-tum Sén-su-um
Pro-ce-dén-ti ab u-tró-que Cóm-par sit

de-fé-ctu-i.
lau-dá-ti-o.   A-men.

MODE IV

Gloria Patri

Gló-ri-a Pá-tri, et Fí-li-o,   et Spí-ri-tu-i Sán-cto

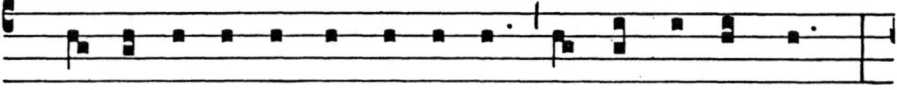

Sí-cut é-rat in prin-cí-pi-o,   et nunc, et sem-per,

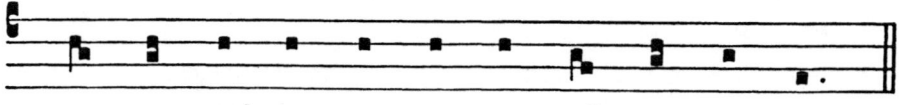

et in saé-cu-la sae-cu-ló-rum. A-men.

MODE V

Tantum Ergo

1. Tan-tum er-go Sa-cra-mén-tum / Ve-ne-ré-mur cér-nu-i: / Et an-tí-quum do-cu-mén-tum / Nó-vo cé-dat rí-tu-i: / Praé-stet fi-des sup-ple-mén-tum / Sén-su-um de-fé-ctu-i.

2. Ge-ni-tó-ri, Ge-ni-tó-que / Laus et ju-bi-lá-ti-o, / Sá-lus, hó-nor, vír-tus quo-que / Sit et be-ne-dí-cti-o: / Pro-ce-dén-ti ab u-tró-que / Cóm-par sit lau-dá-ti-o. A-men.

AIDS TO MODE VI

QUESTIONS

1. What neums appear in this hymn which were not in the preceding ones?

2. What is the final in this mode? What is the dominant?

3. Is this an authentic or a plagal mode?

PRESENTATION OF THE MODES

Ave Verum

[*A chant in honor of the Blessed Sacrament (Thirteenth Century).*]

Hail, true Body, born
Of the Virgin Mary,
Who didst truly suffer and die
On the Cross for man,
From Whose pierced side
Flowed Blood and water,
May we receive Thee, a foretaste of Heaven,
When we are in the agony of death.
O gentle, O loving,
O sweet Jesus, Son of Mary.

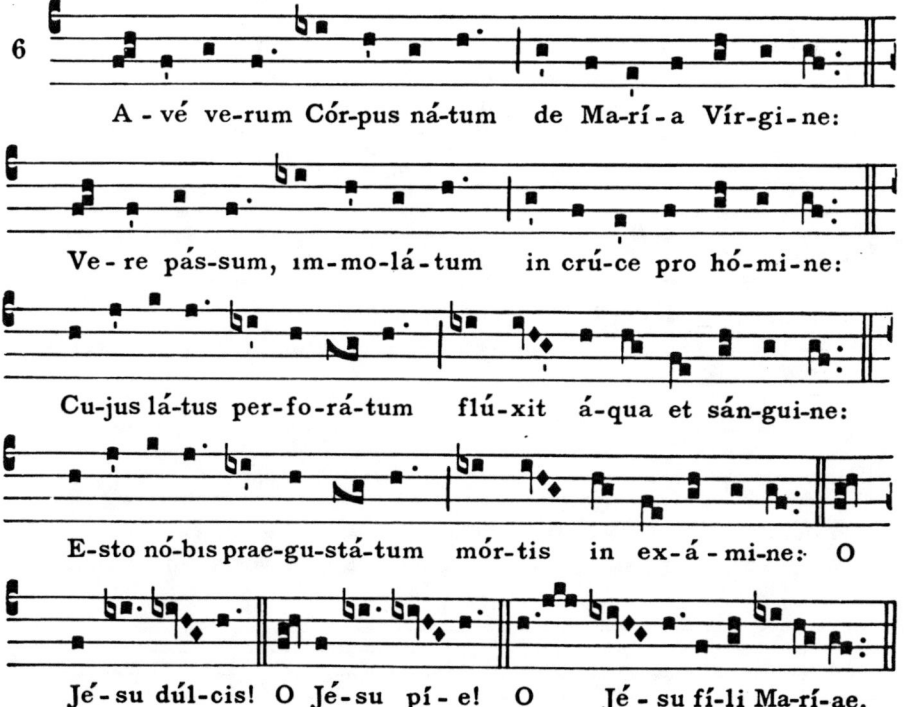

Accidental. The only accidental ever used in Gregorian Chant is flat 7 (*Te*). You will notice that the flat is not made as it is in modern music.

MODE VII

Panis Angelicus

[*A hymn in honor of the Blessed Sacrament, written by Saint Thomas Aquinas.*]

The Bread of Angels becomes the bread of men.
The Bread of Heaven fulfills the prophetic types.
O wondrous truth! The poor, the lowly,
And the slave upon their Master feed.

Thee, Godhead, One and Three, we pray,
Come Thou to visit us, as we our homage pay.
Be thine the path, and Thou our guide, as we journey
To the light where Thou dost dwell.

1. Pá-nis an-gé-li-cus fit pá-nis hó-mi-num; Dat pá-nis caé-li-cus fi-gú-ris
2. Te tri-na Dé-i-tas ú - na-que pó-sci-mus, Sic nos tu ví-si-ta si-cut te

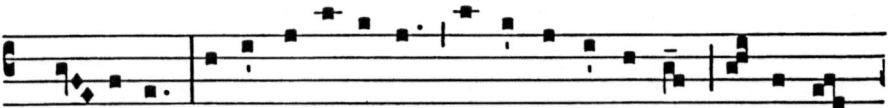

tér-mi-num: O res mi-rá-bi-lis! man-dú-cat Dó-mi-num Paú-per, sér -
có - li-mus: Per tú-as sé-mi-tas duc nos quo tén-di-mus Ad lu-cem

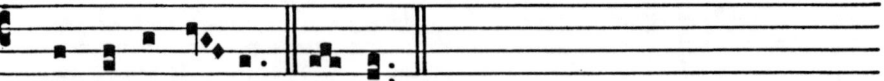

vus, et hú-mi - lis.
quam in-há-bi - tas.   A - men.

Name the new *final* and *dominant*.

MODE VIII

Pacificus

[*An anthem for the feast of Christ the King.*]

He shall be called Peacemaker,
And His throne shall be established forever.

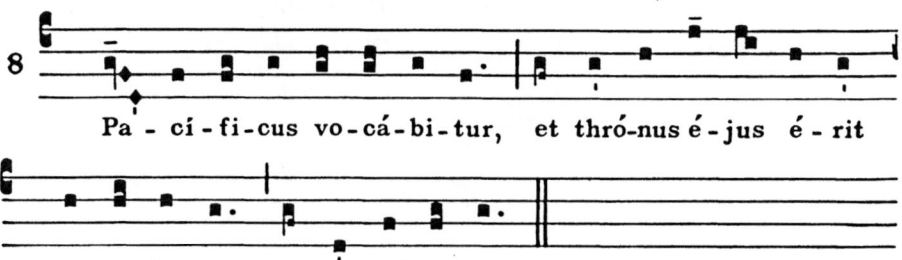

Pa - ci - fi - cus vo - cá - bi - tur, et thró - nus é - jus é - rit

fir - mis - si - mus in per - pé - tu - um.

TRANSPOSITION OF THE MODES

In modern music when a melody is changed from one key to another, it is said to be transposed, the purpose of transposition being to raise or lower the pitch of the melody. When this takes place, the key signature is changed accordingly, and the melody is sung with the same syllables.

In the chant there is no key signature, and so one must be guided entirely by the *clefs*. A transposition may occur for apparently no reason, as in the following hymn *O filii*. The second mode, as explained before, is generally written with the *Fa* clef on the third line. In this case the melody would start on *Re*, thus:

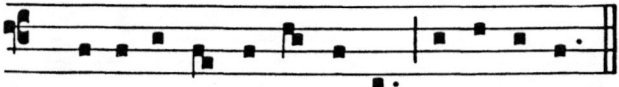

Sing this phrase, then change *Re* to *La* and sing the hymn as it is written, with the *Do* clef on the third line. You will discover that there is no change whatever in the pitch of the melody or in the arrangement of the tones, but the final is now *La* instead of *Re*, and the dominant is *Do*.

In modes such as I, III, IV, VI, and VIII, where the *Do* clef is regularly on the fourth line, the clef is often moved to the third, or even to the second line, in order that the melody may be kept within the limits of the staff whenever possible.

For this same reason the *Do* clef in modes V and VII is often moved from the third line, where it regularly appears, to the fourth line. One has only to remember the location of *Do*, which is always fixed by the position of the *Do* clef.

O Filii

[*A hymn for Easter, written in the fifteenth century.*]

O sons and daughters,
The King of Heaven, the King of glory,
Hath risen from the dead today.

And the morning of the first day after the sabbath
His disciples drew near
The door of the tomb.

And Mary Magdalene
And Mary, the mother of Jacob and Salome,
Came to anoint the body.

An angel sitting, clad in white,
Announced to the women:
The Lord is in Galilee.

On this most holy feast
Let there be praise and song of joy.
Let us bless the Lord!

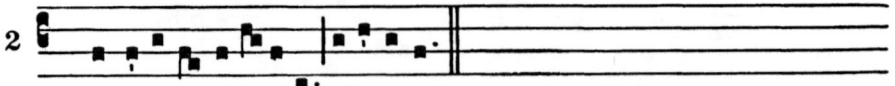

Al-le-lú-ia, al-le-lú-ia, al-le-lú-ia. *Repeat Alleluias after each stanza.*

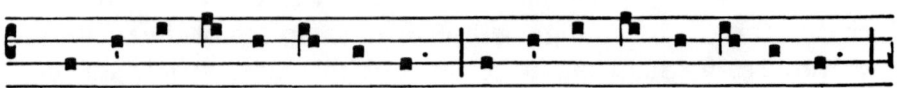

1. O fí - li - i   et   fí - li - ae, Rex cae-lé-stis, Rex gló-ri - ae,

PRESENTATION OF THE MODES

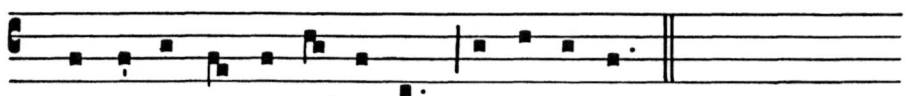

Mór-te sur-ré-xit hó-di-e,   Al-le-lú-ia.

2. Et mane príma sábbati,
   Ad óstium monuménti
   Accessérunt discípuli, allelúia.

3. Et María Magdaléne,
   Et Jacóbi et Salóme,
   Venérunt córpus úngere, allelúia.

4. In álbis sédens Angelus
   Praedíxit muliéribus:
   In Galiláea est Dóminus, allelúia.

5. In hoc fésto sanctíssimo
   Sit laus et jubilátio,
   Benedicámus Dómino, allelúia.

v
REPERTORY

SELECTIONS IN THIS CHAPTER

Ave Maria · Page 37
The Asperges · Page 37   Vidi Aquam · Page 39

I · DURING EASTERTIDE
Lux et origo · Page 41
Kyrie, 41 · Gloria, 41 · Sanctus, 43 · Agnus Dei, 43

II · FOR SOLEMN FEASTS
Kyrie fons bonitatis · Page 44
Kyrie, 44 · Gloria, 44 · Sanctus, 46 · Agnus Dei, 47

VIII · FOR DOUBLE FEASTS
De Angelis · Page 47
Kyrie, 47 · Gloria, 48 · Sanctus, 50 · Agnus Dei, 50

FOR FEASTS OF THE BLESSED VIRGIN
IX · Cum jubilo · Page 51
Kyrie, 51 · Gloria, 52 · Sanctus, 53 · Agnus Dei, 54

X · Alme Pater · Page 55
Kyrie, 55 · Gloria, 55 · Sanctus, 57 · Agnus Dei, 57

XI · FOR SUNDAYS THROUGHOUT THE YEAR
Orbis factor · Page 58
Kyrie, 58 · Gloria, 58 · Sanctus, 60 · Agnus Dei, 61

XVII · FOR SUNDAYS OF ADVENT AND LENT
Kyrie, 61 · Sanctus, 61 · Agnus Dei, 62

Credo I · Page 63   Credo III · Page 66

REPERTORY

RESPONSES AT HIGH MASS

Responses · Page 69　　　At the Gospel · Page 70

At the Preface
Solemn Tone for Solemn Feasts · Page 70
Simple Tone for Simple Feasts and Ferial Days · Page 70

At the Pater Noster · Page 71
Before the Agnus Dei · Page 71
At the Pontifical Blessing · Page 72

At the End of Mass
During Eastertide · Page 72
On Solemn Feasts · Page 72
On Feasts of the Blessed Virgin · Page 73
On Sundays throughout the Year · Page 73
On Simple Feasts · Page 73

Gloria (Ambrosian) · Page 73

MASS FOR THE DEAD

Introit · Page 75
Sequence · Page 76
Offertory · Page 79
Communion · Page 82
Absolution after Mass · Page 82

Rorate Caeli (Introit) · Page 84　　Rorate Caeli (Hymn) · Page 85
Puer Natus in Bethlehem · Page 88
Puer Nobis Nascitur · Page 90
Dominus Dixit ad Me · Page 90

ANTIPHON

Hodie Christus · Page 91

Quem Vidistis · Page 92
O Admirabile Commercium · Page 92
Attende Domine · Page 93　　　Stabat Mater · Page 94

Pueri Hebraeorum (Antiphon) · Page 96
Pueri Hebraeorum · Page 97
Gloria, Laus, et Honor · Page 97
Crucem Tuam Adoramus · Page 99
Vexilla Regis · Page 100
O Vos Omnes · Page 102
Vespere · Page 103
Pascha Nostrum · Page 103
Surrexit Dominus Vere · Page 104
Regina Caeli · Page 104
Viri Galilaei · Page 105
Repleti Sunt · Page 105
Veni Sancte Spiritus · Page 106
Veni Creator · Page 107
O Sacrum Convivium · Page 110
Adoro Te · Page 110
Ecce Panis Angelorum · Page 113
Pange Lingua · Page 114
O Salutaris Hostia · Page 116
O Salutaris · Page 117
O Salutaris · Page 117
O Salutaris · Page 118
Tantum Ergo · Page 118
Salva Nos · Page 119
Sancti Angeli · Page 120
Beati Mundo · Page 120
O Quam Gloriosum Est Regnum · Page 121
Creator Alme Siderum · Page 122
Jesu Dulcis Memoria · Page 122
Te Joseph Celebrent · Page 124
Beata Mater · Page 125
Alma Redemptoris · Page 126
Ave Regina · Page 127
Salve Regina · Page 127
Ave Maris Stella · Page 129
Salve Mater · Page 130

Ave Maria

Locate a pressus which is formed by the meeting of a single punctum and a podatus. These two notes on the same degree of the staff are to be sung as one note. The pressus is always equivalent to a tie.

The Asperges

Thou shalt sprinkle me with hyssop, O Lord,
And I shall be cleansed.
Thou shalt wash me,
And I shall be made whiter than snow.
Have mercy on me, O God,
According to Thy great mercy.

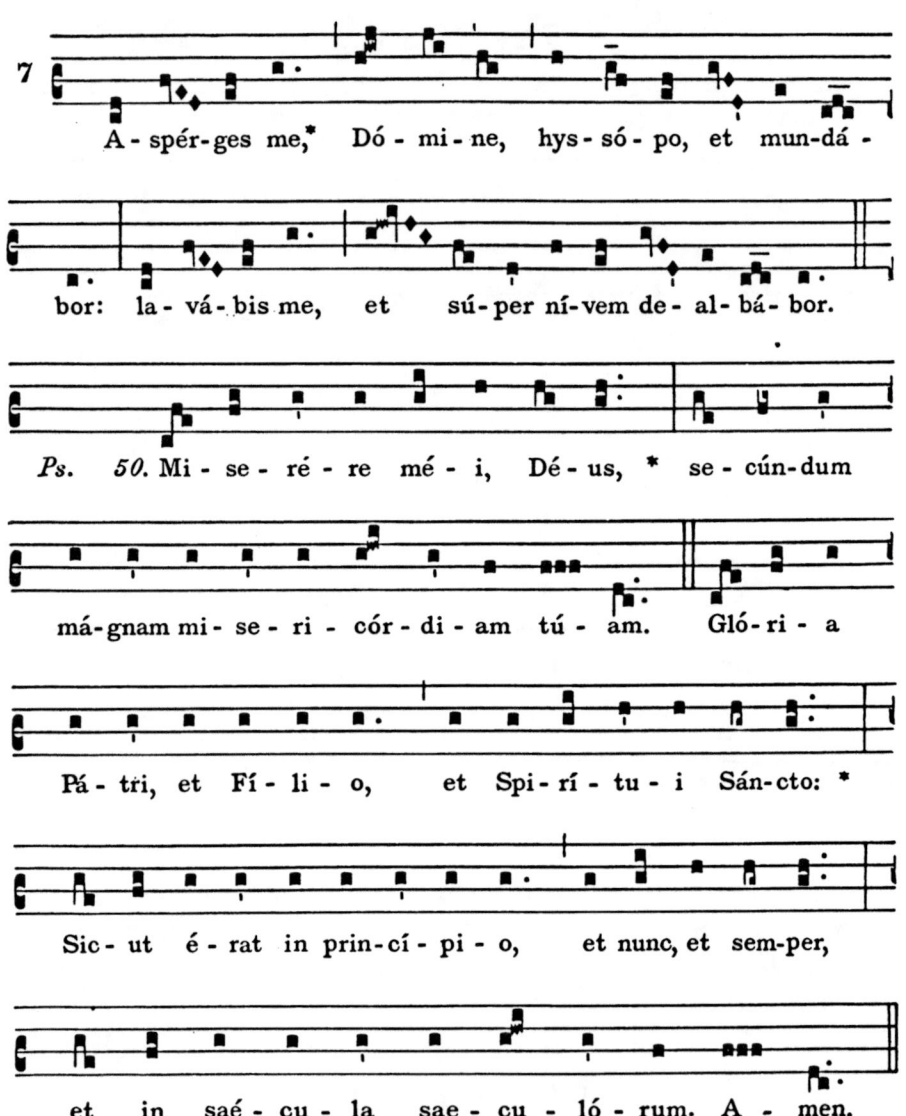

Repeat the antiphon *Asperges me*.

On Passion Sunday and Palm Sunday the *Gloria Patri* is not sung, but the antiphon *Asperges me* is repeated immediately after the psalm.

℣.[1] Osténde nóbis, Dómine, misericórdiam túam. (*In Eastertide add:* Allelúia).
℟. Et salutáre túum da nóbis. (Allelúia).
℣. Dómine exáudi oratiónem méam.
℟. Et clámor méus ad te véniat.
℣. Dóminus vobíscum.
℟. Et cum spíritu túo.

(Prayer) Response, Amen.

Translation of the foregoing versicles and responses:

℣. Show us, Lord, Thy mercy.
℟. And grant us the salvation that comes from Thee.
℣. Lord, hear and answer my prayer.
℟. And let my cry come unto Thee.
℣. The Lord be with you.
℟. And with Thy spirit.

Vidi Aquam

[*From Easter Sunday to Pentecost inclusive*]

I saw water coming forth
From the temple,
On the right side, alleluia,
And all, to whom this water came,
Were healed, and will sing, alleluia, alleluia.
Give praise to the Lord,
For he is good;
For His mercy endureth forever.

[1] This is a sign which stands for the word *versicle*. A versicle is a short sentence sung by the priest and followed by a response from the choir or congregation. R. or ℟. stands for the word *response*.

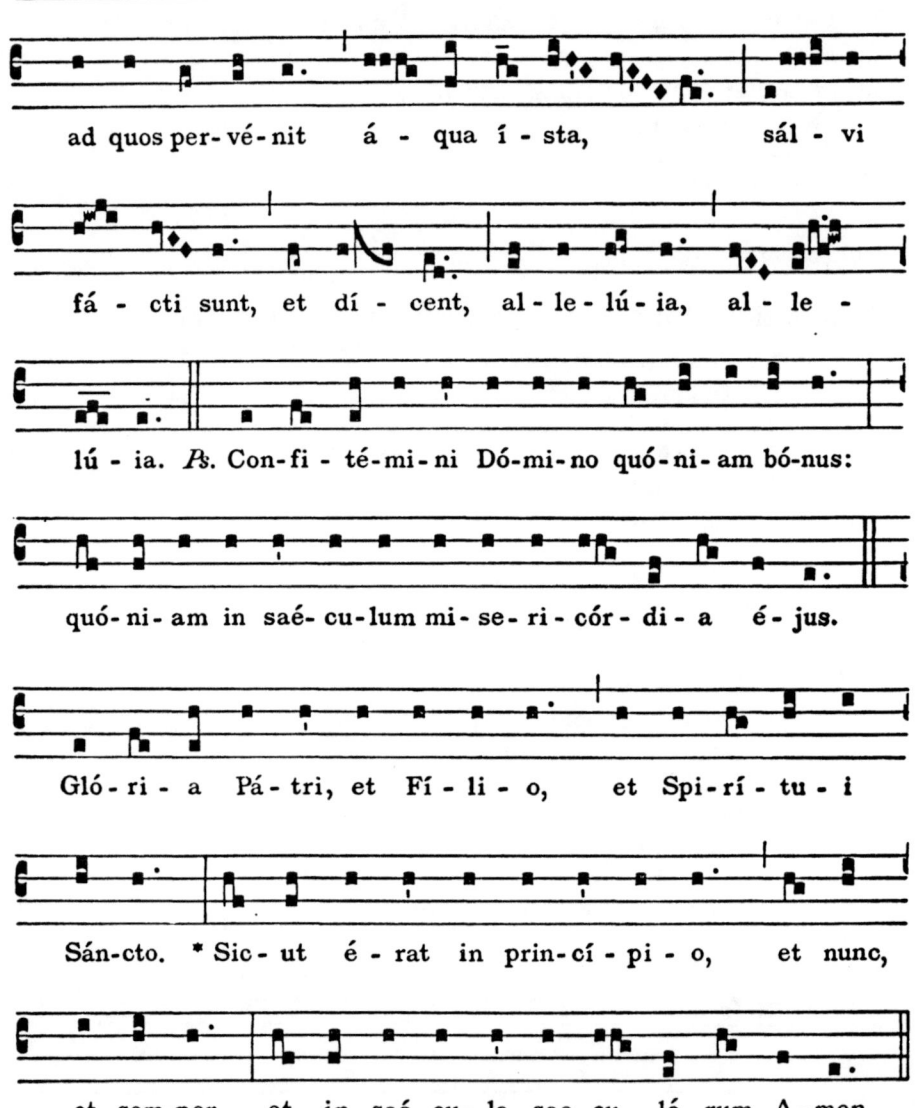

Repeat from the beginning to *Ps.*

I · DURING EASTERTIDE

Lux et origo (*Light and beginning*)

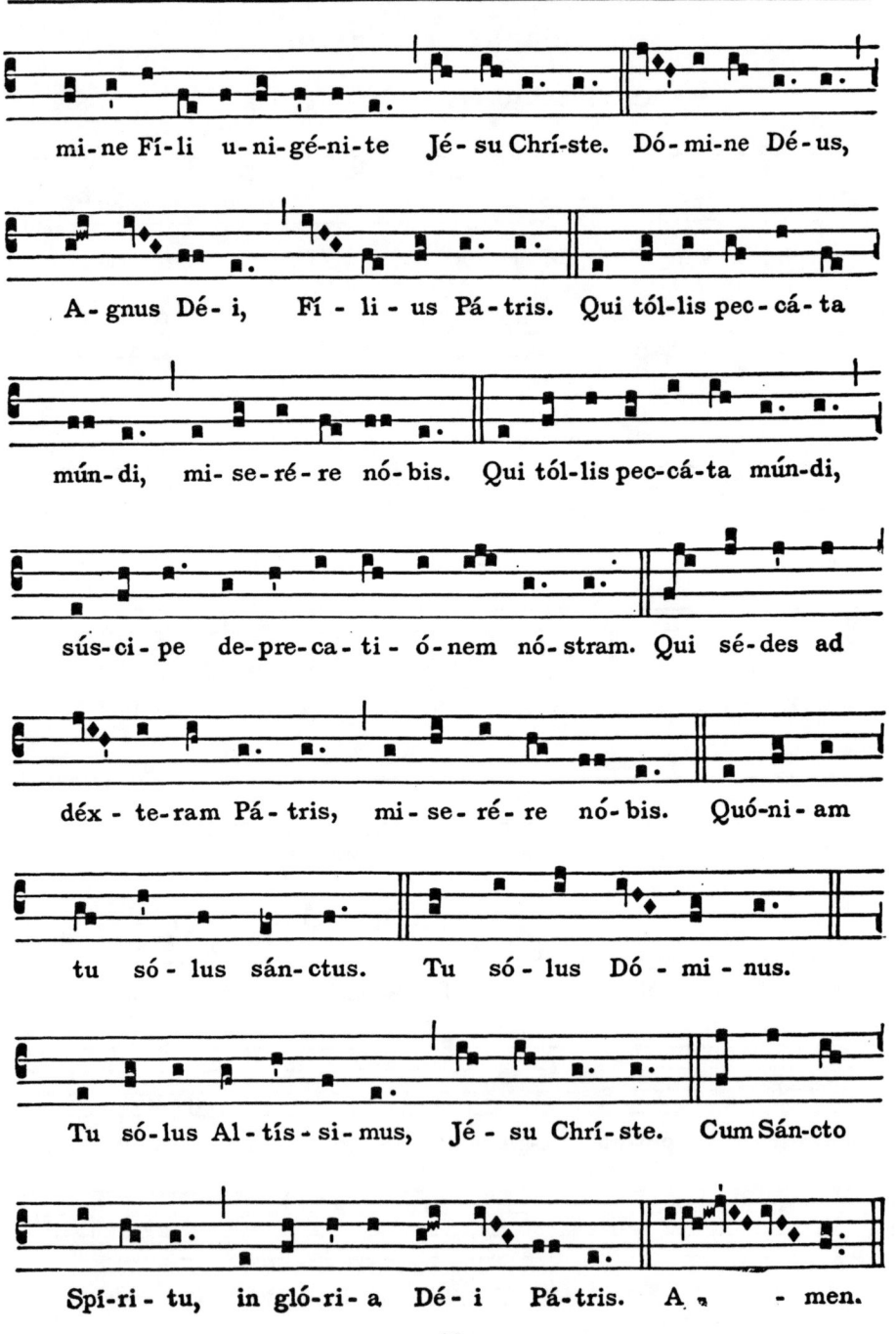

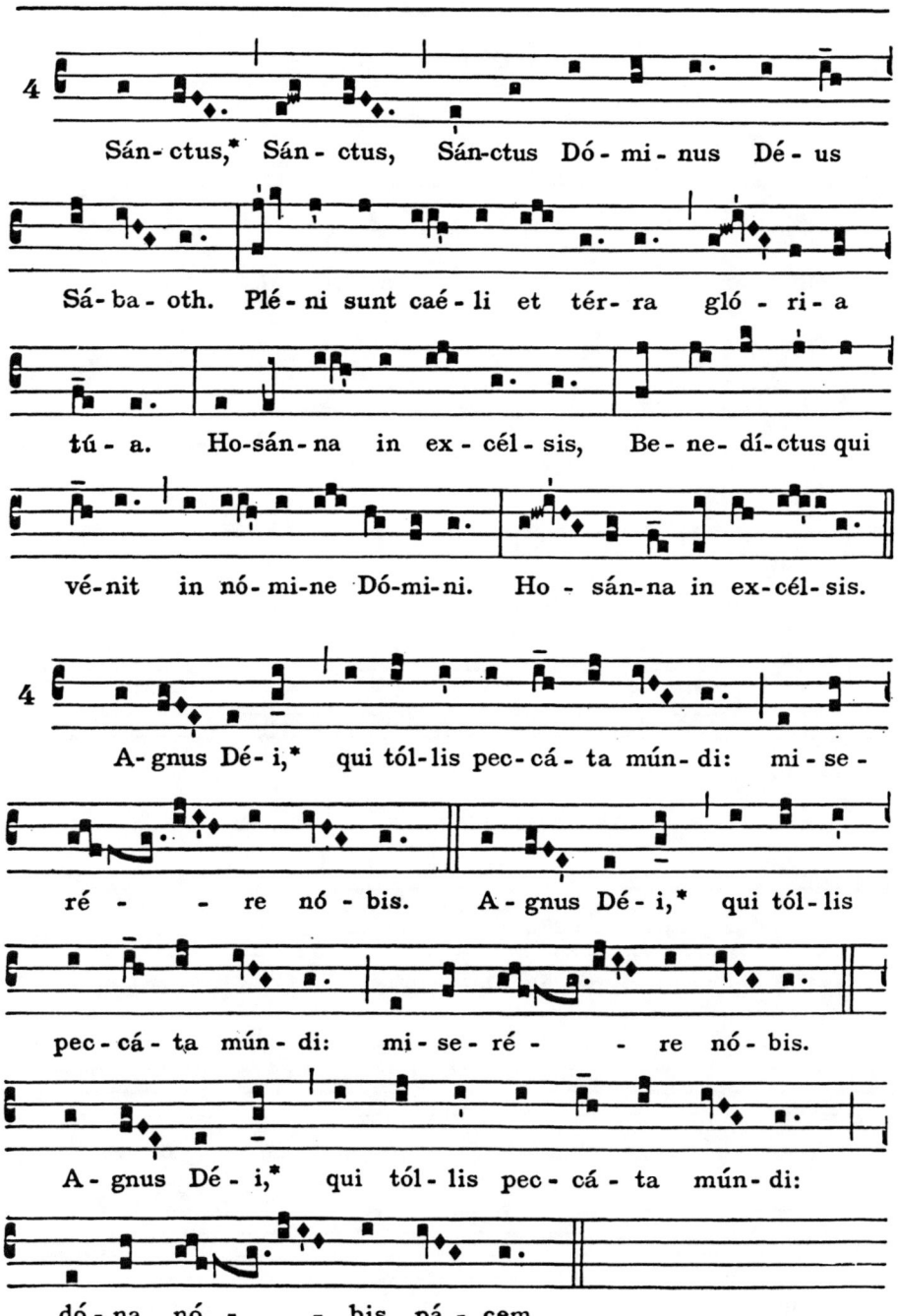

II · FOR SOLEMN FEASTS

Kyrie fons bonitatis (*Fount of Goodness*)

Ký-ri-e * e-lé-i-son. *III.* Chrí-ste
e-lé-i-son. *III.* Ký-ri-e
e-lé-i-son. *II.* Ký-ri-e *
* e-lé-i-son.

Gló-ri-a in ex-cél-sis Dé-o. Et in tér-ra pax ho-mí-ni-bus bó-nae vo-lun-tá-tis. Lau-dá-mus te. Be-ne-dí-ci-mus te. A-do-rá-mus te. Glo-ri-fi-cá-mus te.

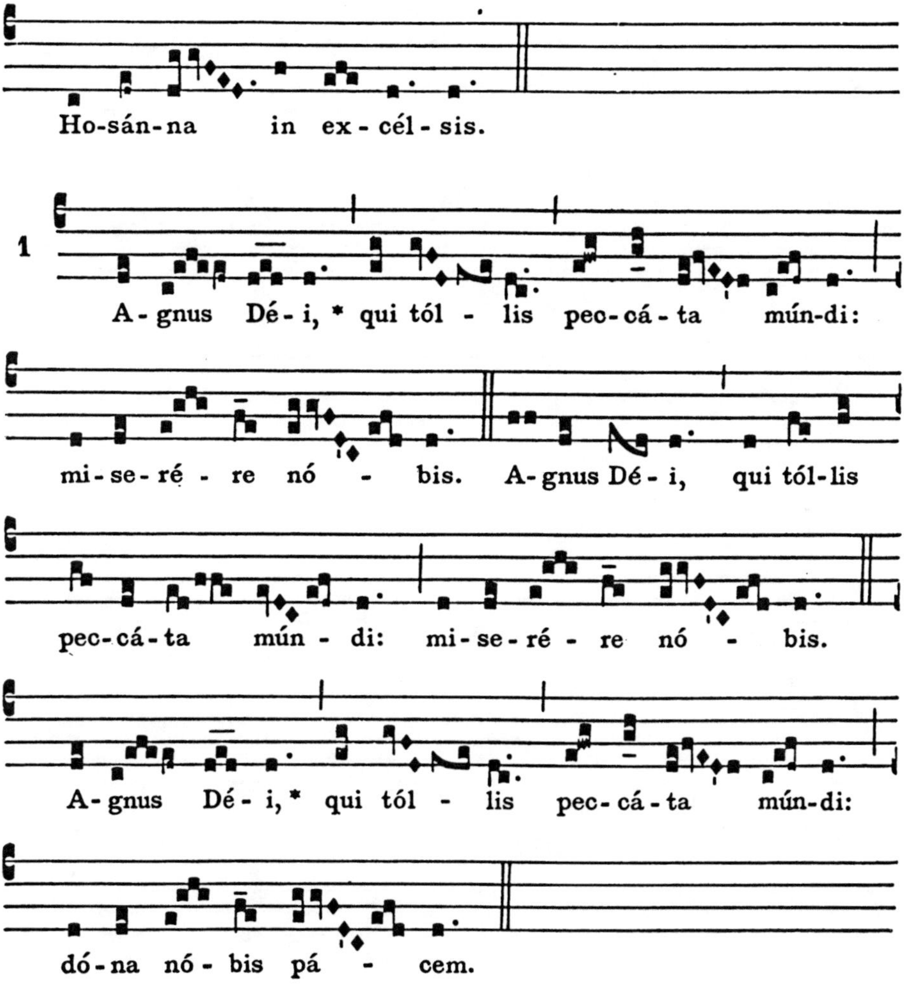

Ho-sán-na in ex-cél-sis.

1. A-gnus Dé-i, * qui tól-lis pec-cá-ta mún-di: mi-se-ré-re nó-bis. A-gnus Dé-i, qui tól-lis pec-cá-ta mún-di: mi-se-ré-re nó-bis. A-gnus Dé-i, * qui tól-lis pec-cá-ta mún-di: dó-na nó-bis pá-cem.

VIII · FOR DOUBLE FEASTS

De Angelis (*Mass of the Angels*)

5. Ký-ri-e * e-lé-i-son. *III.* Chrí-ste

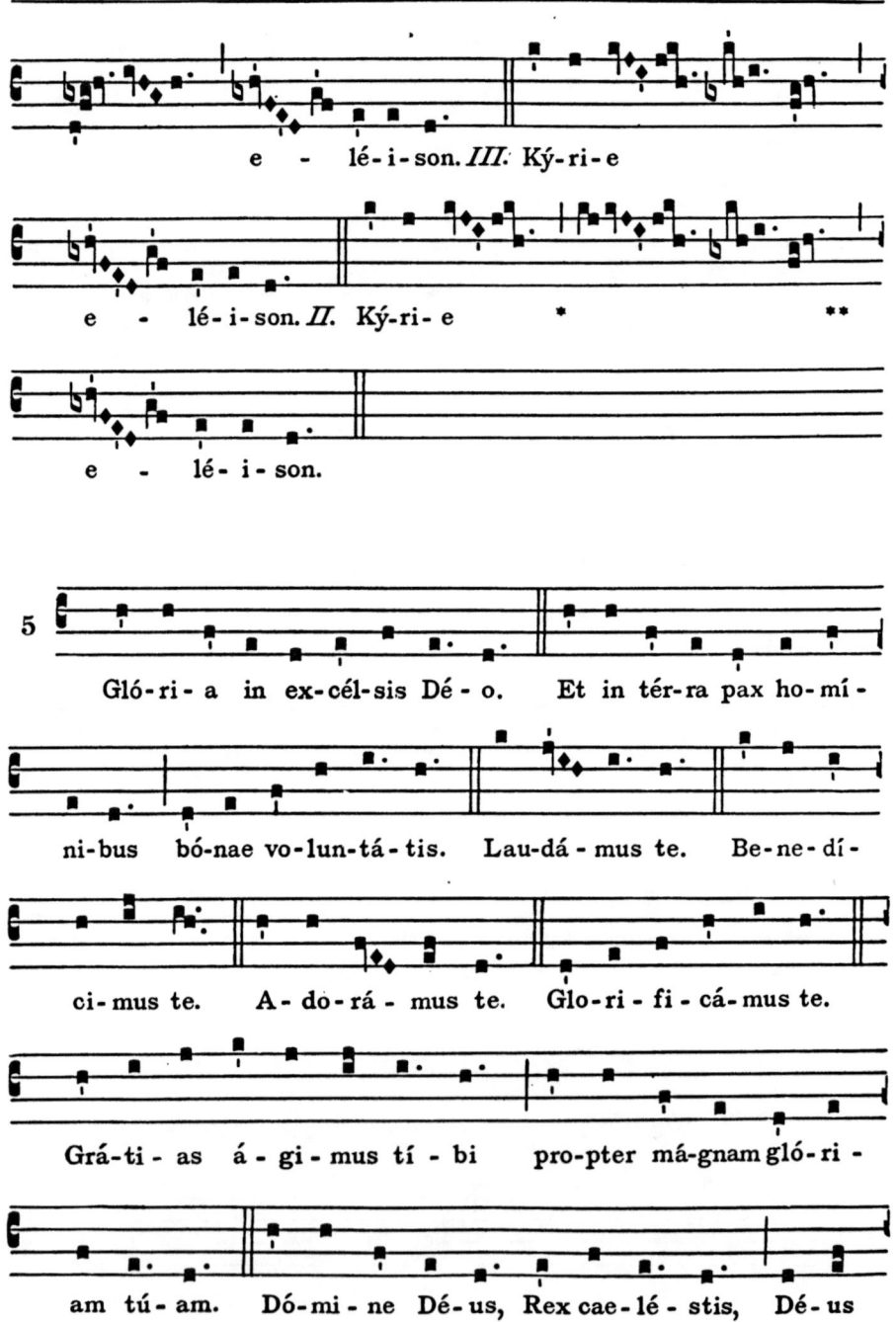

FOR FEASTS OF THE BLESSED VIRGIN

IX
Cum jubilo (*With a Song of Joy*)

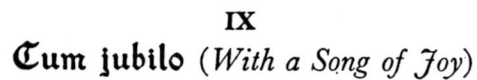

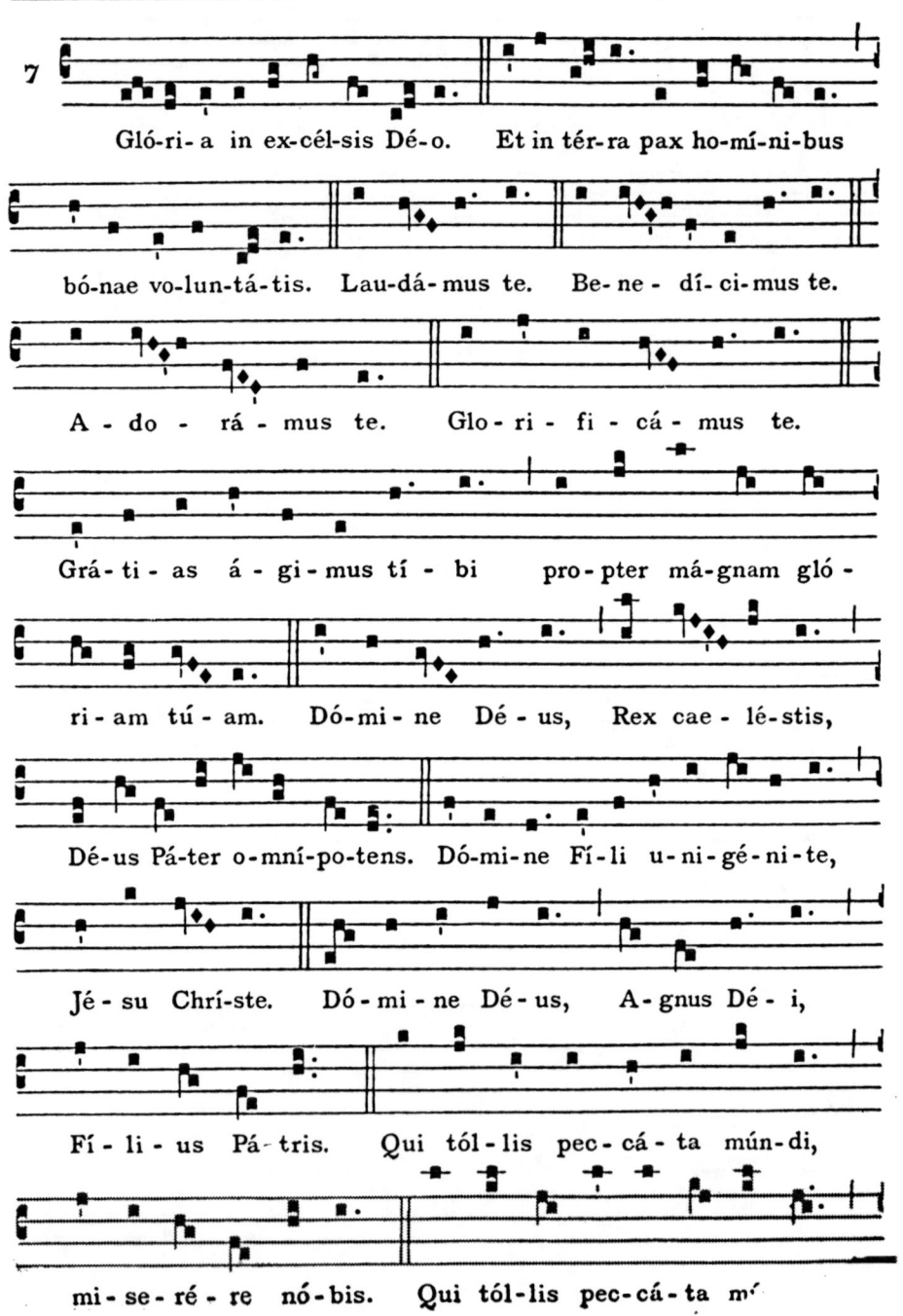

XI · FOR SUNDAYS THROUGHOUT THE YEAR

Orbis factor (*Maker of the World*)

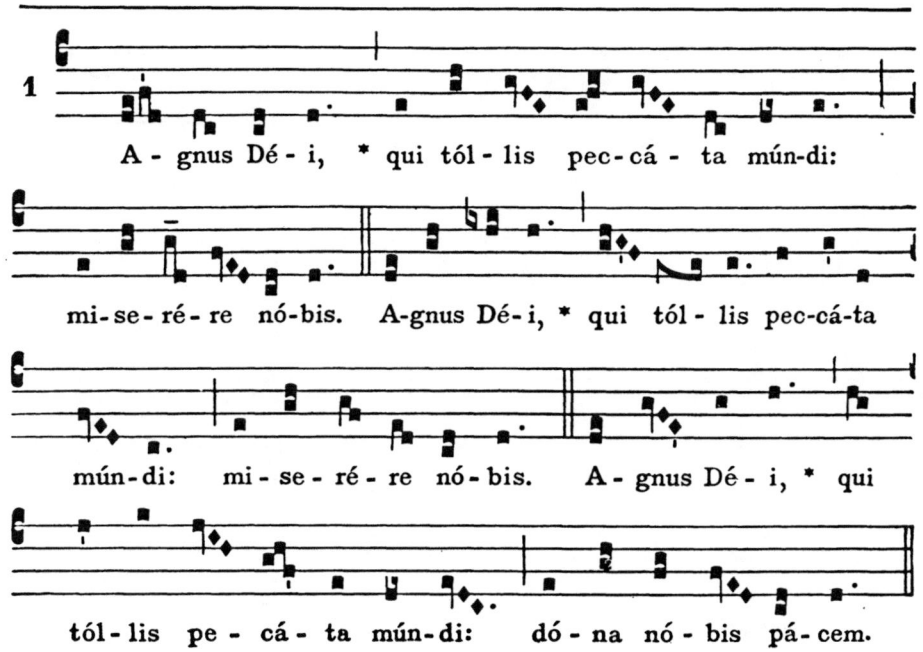

1. A‑gnus Dé‑i, * qui tól‑lis pec‑cá‑ta mún‑di: mi‑se‑ré‑re nó‑bis. A‑gnus Dé‑i, * qui tól‑lis pec‑cá‑ta mún‑di: mi‑se‑ré‑re nó‑bis. A‑gnus Dé‑i, * qui tól‑lis pe‑cá‑ta mún‑di: dó‑na nó‑bis pá‑cem.

XVII · FOR SUNDAYS OF ADVENT AND LENT

6. Ký‑ri‑e * e‑lé‑i‑son. III. Chrí‑ste e‑lé‑i‑son. III. Ký‑ri‑e e‑lé‑i‑son. II. Ký‑ri‑e * e‑lé‑i‑son.

5. Sán‑ctus, * Sán‑ctus, Sán‑ctus Dó‑mi‑nus Dé‑us

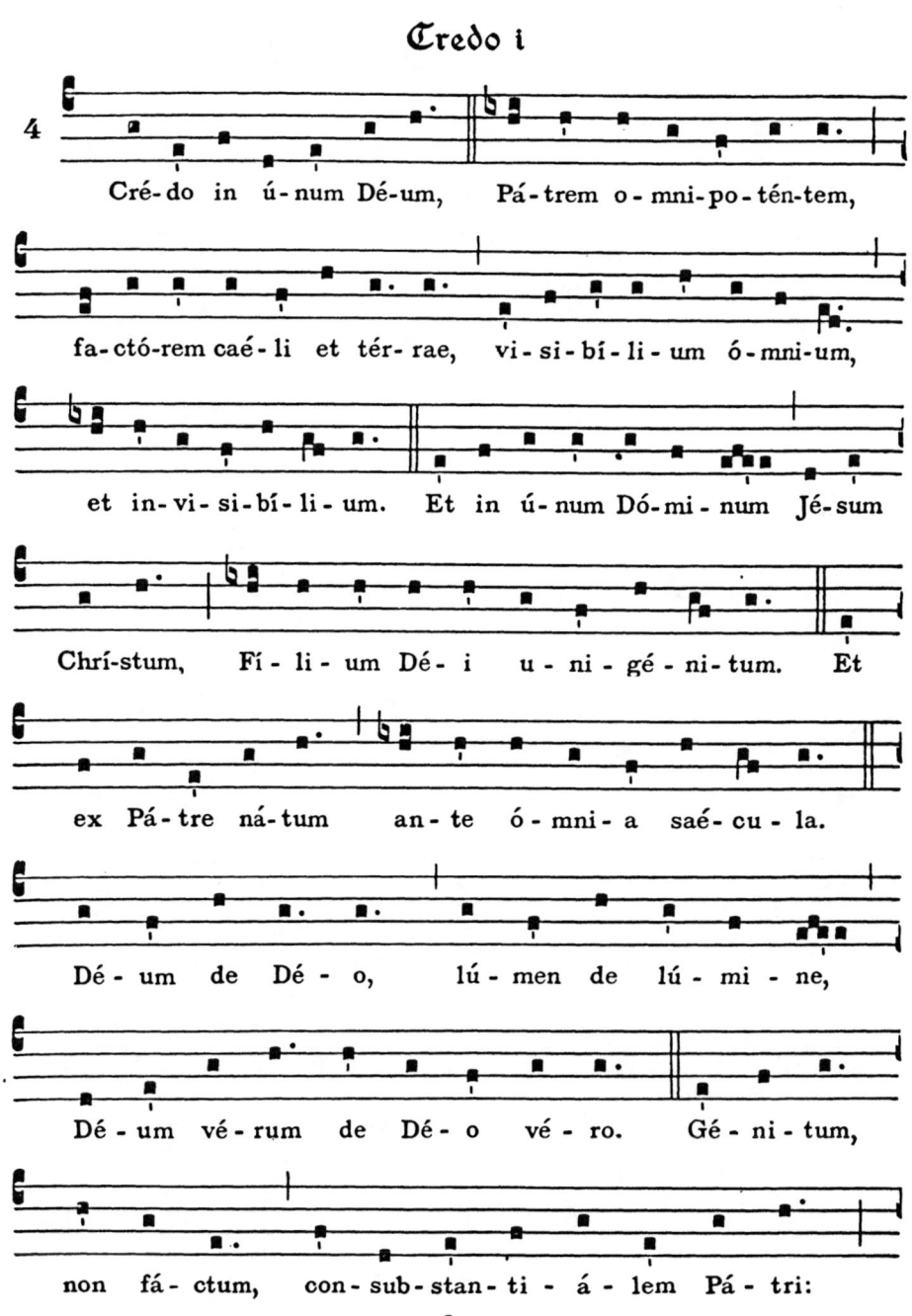

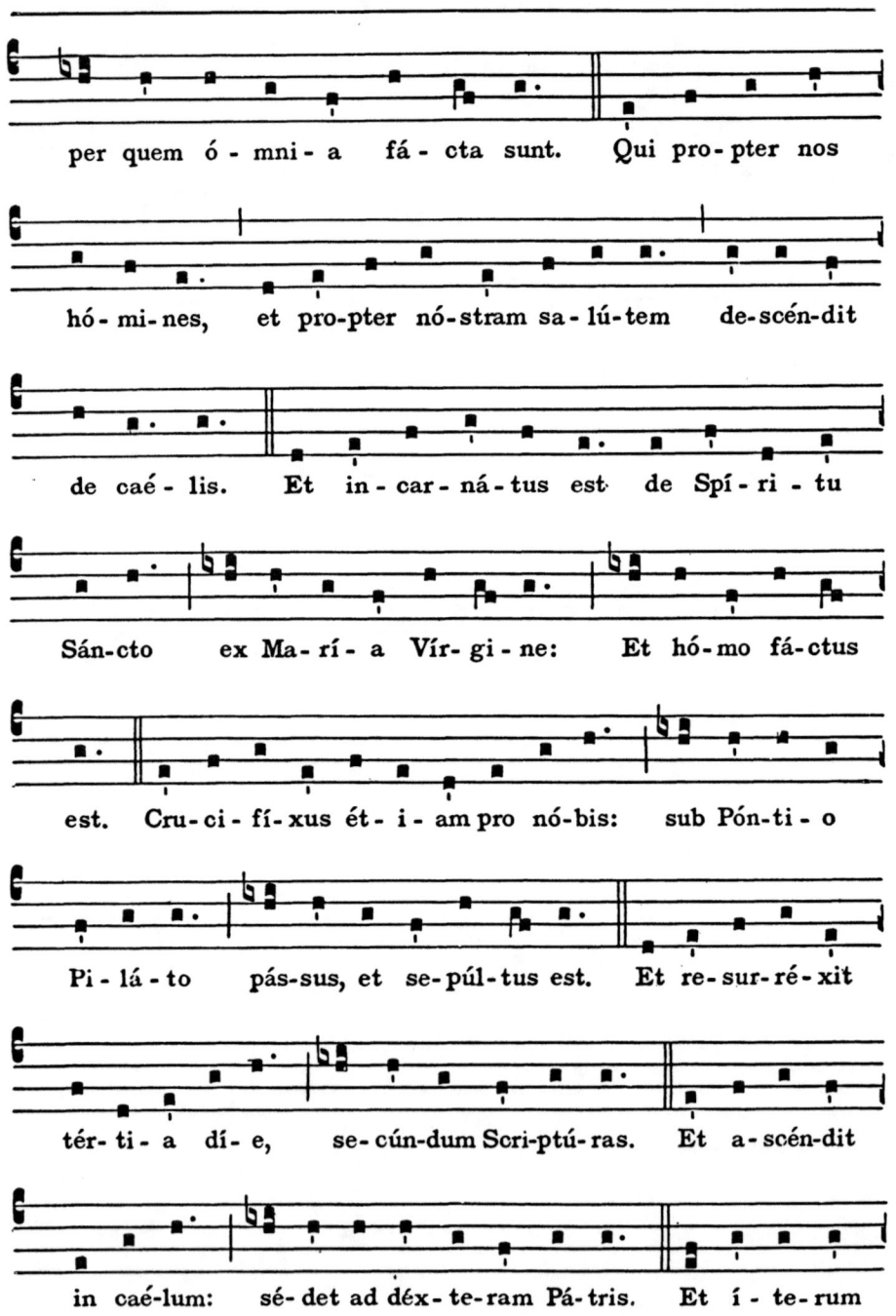

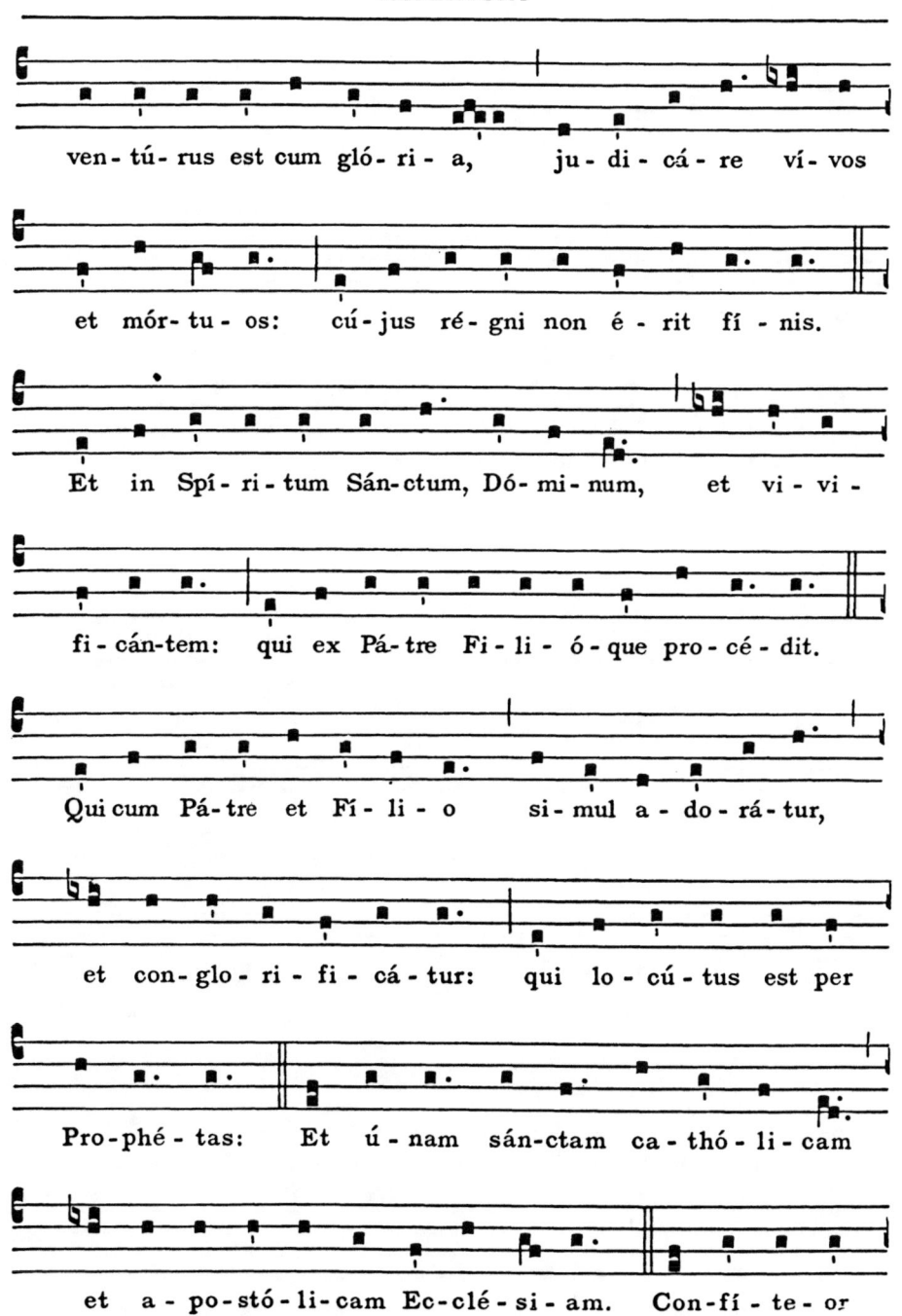

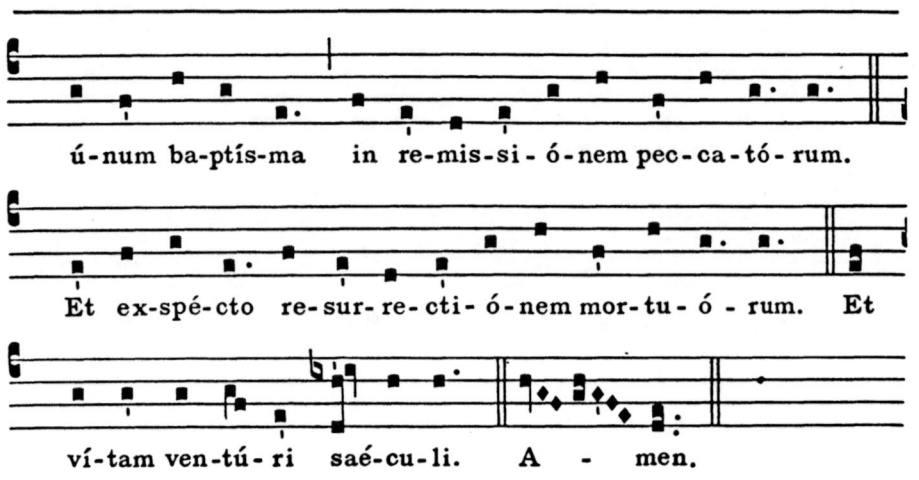

ú-num ba-ptís-ma in re-mis-si- ó-nem pec-ca-tó-rum.

Et ex-spé-cto re-sur-re-cti- ó-nem mor-tu- ó - rum. Et

ví-tam ven-tú- ri saé-cu-li. A - men.

Credo iii

5 Cré-do in ú-num Dé- um, Pá-trem o-mni-po-tén-tem, fa-ctó-

rem caé-li et tér-rae, vi- si- bí - li- um ó - mni-um, et

in- vi - si- bí - li- um. Et in ú- num Dó-mi-num Jé-sum Chrí-

stum, Fí-li-um Dé- i u - ni-gé-ni-tum. Et ex Pá-tre ná- tum

an- te ó-mni- a saé - cu-la. Dé-um de Dé- o, lú-men

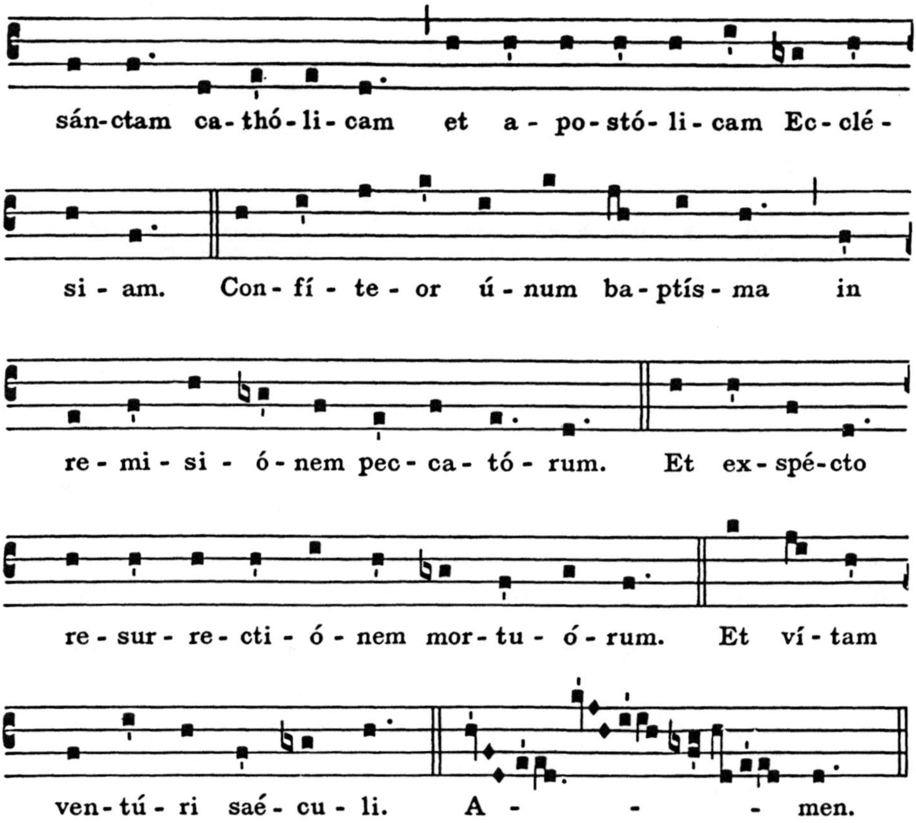

sán-ctam ca-thó-li-cam et a-po-stó-li-cam Ec-clé-si-am. Con-fí-te-or ú-num ba-ptís-ma in re-mi-si-ó-nem pec-ca-tó-rum. Et ex-spé-cto re-sur-re-cti-ó-nem mor-tu-ó-rum. Et ví-tam ven-tú-ri saé-cu-li. A - - - men.

RESPONSES AT HIGH MASS

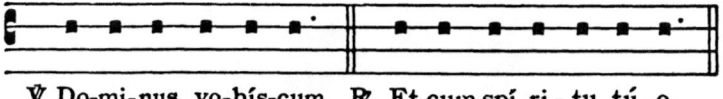

℣. Do-mi-nus vo-bís-cum. ℟. Et cum spí-ri-tu tú-o.

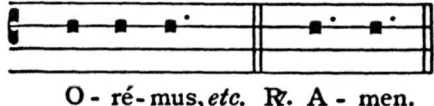

O-ré-mus, *etc.* ℟. A-men.

At the Gospel

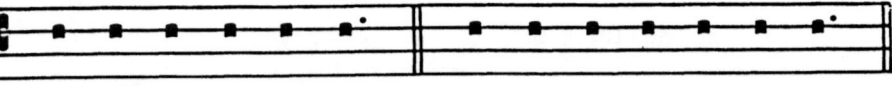

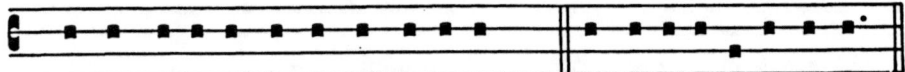

At the Preface

[Solemn Tone, for Solemn Feasts]

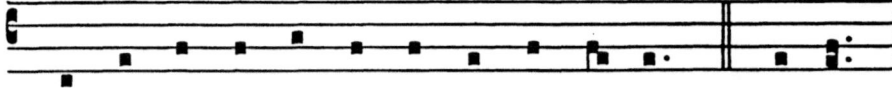

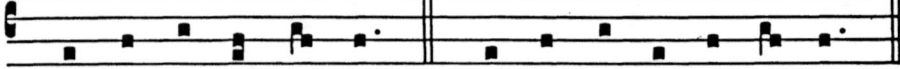

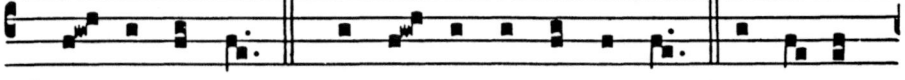

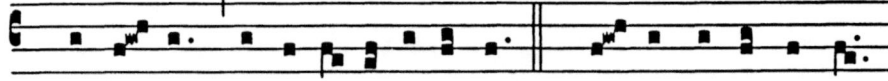

At the Preface

*[Simple Tone, for Simple Feasts and Ferial Days
(Days on which no saint's feast occurs)]*

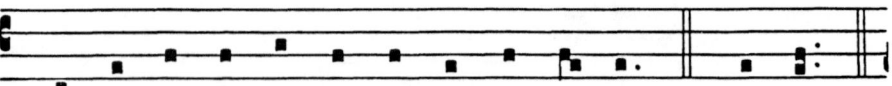

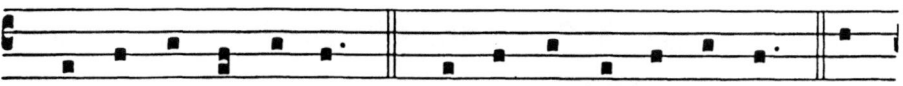
℣. Dó-mi-nus vo-bís-cum. ℟. Et cum spí-ri-tu tú-o. ℣. Sur-

sum cór-da. ℟. Ha-bé-mus ad Dó-mi-num. ℣. Grá-ti-as

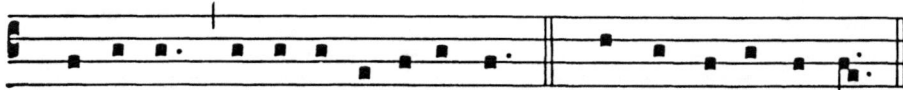
a-gá-mus Dó-mi-no Dé-o nó-stro. ℟. Dí-gnum et jús-tum est.

At the Pater Noster

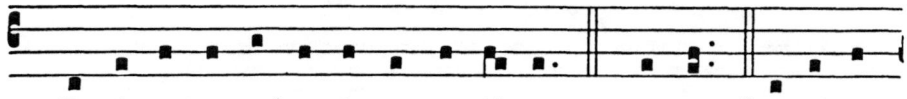
Per ó-mni-a saé-cu-la sae-cu-ló-rum. ℟. A-men. ℣. Et ne nos

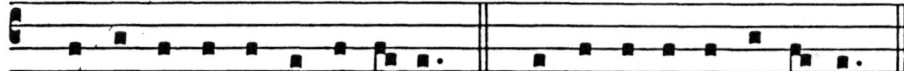
in-dú-cas in ten-ta-ti-ó-nem. ℟. Sed lí-be-ra nos a má-lo.

Before the Agnus Dei

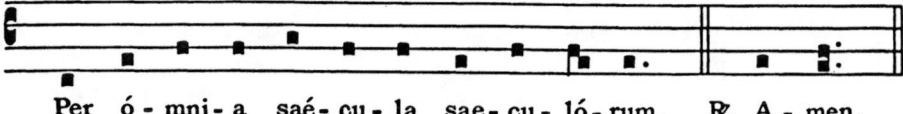
Per ó-mni-a saé-cu-la sae-cu-ló-rum. ℟. A-men.

℣. Pax Dó-mi-ni sit sem-per vo-bís-cum. ℟. Et cum spí-ri-tu tu-o.

At the Pontifical Blessing

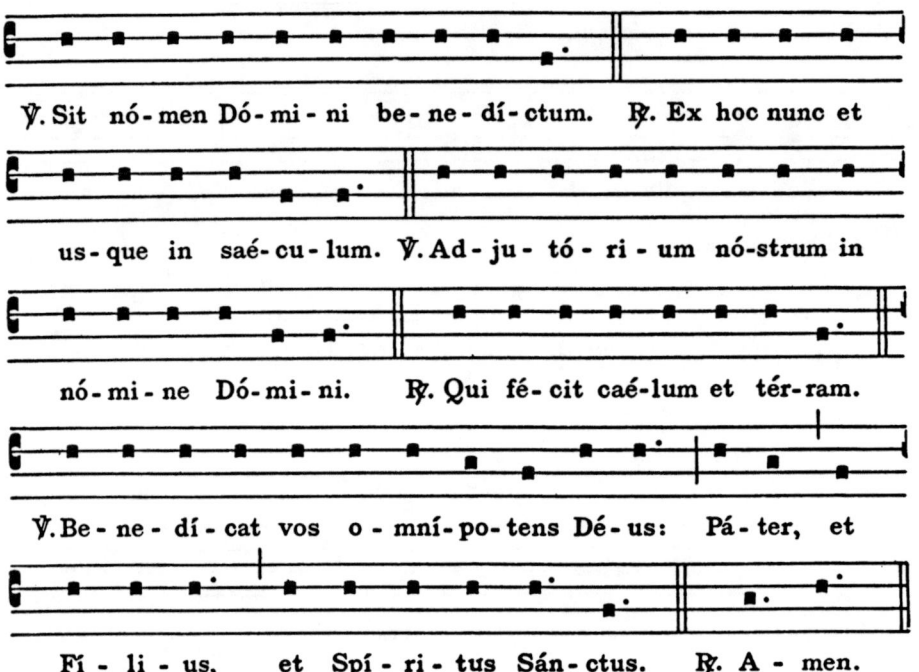

℣. Sit nó-men Dó-mi-ni be-ne-dí-ctum. ℟. Ex hoc nunc et us-que in saé-cu-lum. ℣. Ad-ju-tó-ri-um nó-strum in nó-mi-ne Dó-mi-ni. ℟. Qui fé-cit caé-lum et tér-ram. ℣. Be-ne-dí-cat vos o-mní-po-tens Dé-us: Pá-ter, et Fí-li-us, et Spí-ri-tus Sán-ctus. ℟. A-men.

At the End of Mass

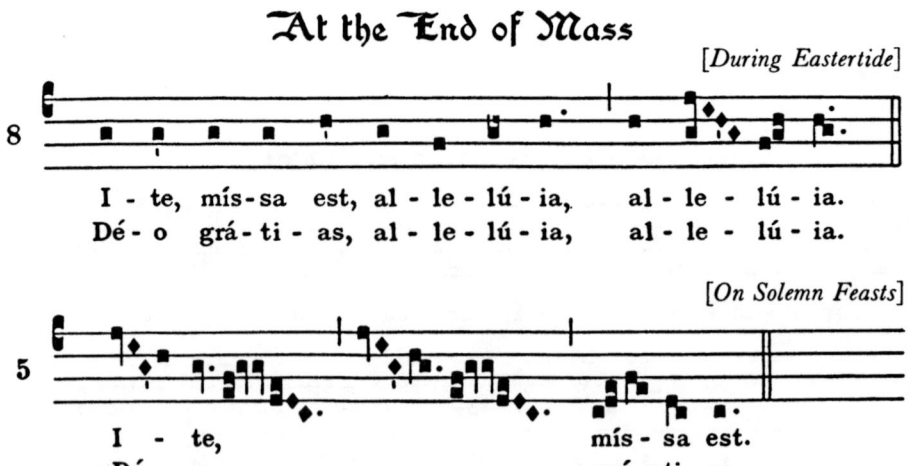

[During Eastertide]

I - te, mís-sa est, al-le-lú-ia, al-le-lú-ia.
Dé-o grá-ti-as, al-le-lú-ia, al-le-lú-ia.

[On Solemn Feasts]

I - te, mís-sa est.
Dé-o grá-ti-as.

Qui sé-des ad déx-te-ram Pá-tris, mi-se-ré-re nó-bis.

Quó-ni-am tu só-lus sán-ctus. Tu só-lus Dó-mi-nus.

Tu só-lus Al-tís-si-mus, Jé-su Chrí-ste.

Cum Sán-cto Spí-ri-tu, in gló-ri-a Dé-i

Pá-tris. ** A - men.

MASS FOR THE DEAD

Introit

Re-qui-em* ae-tér-nam dó-na é-is Dó-mi-ne: et lux per-pé-tu-a lú-ce-at é-is.

Ps. Te dé-cet hým-nus Dé-us in Sí-on, et tí-bi

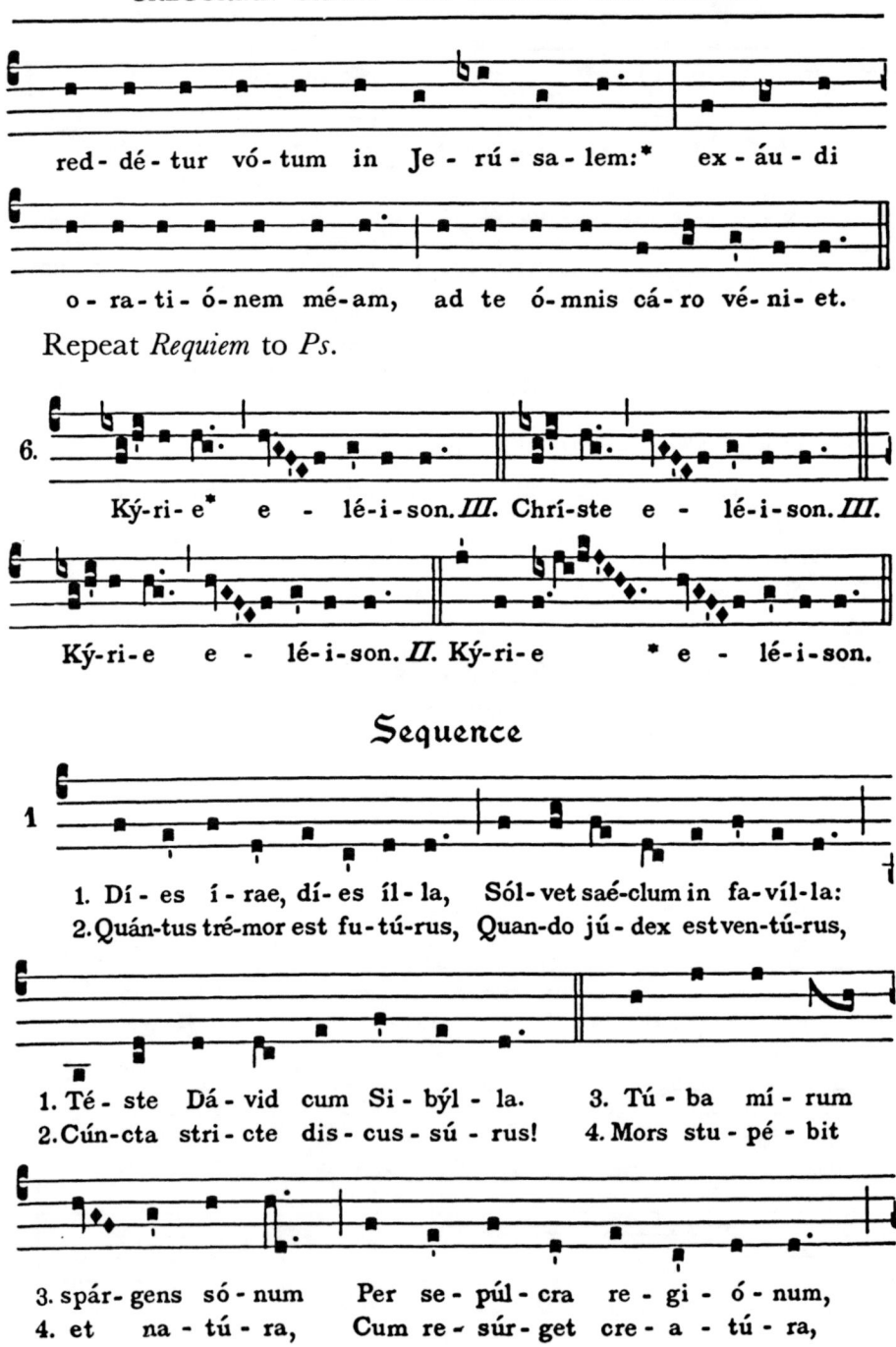

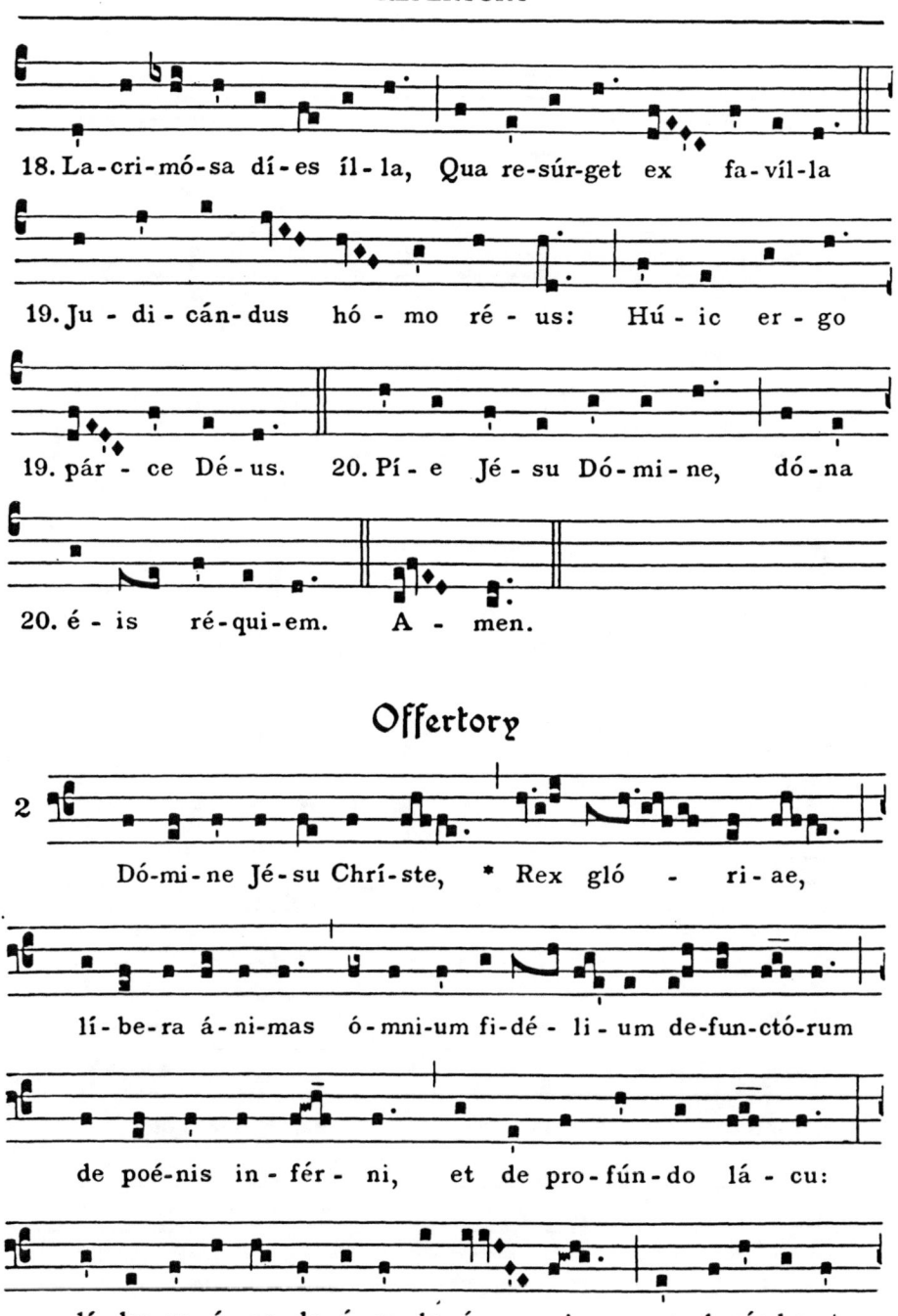

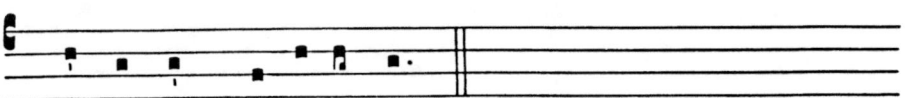

ré- qui- em ** sem-pi-tér-nam.

Communion

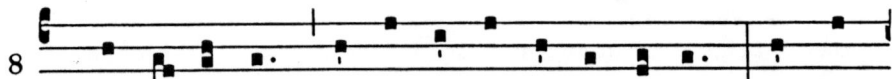

Lux ae- tér- na * lú- ce- at é - is, Dó- mi - ne: * Cum sán-

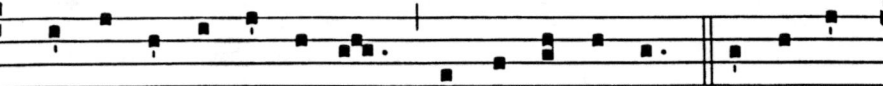

ctis tú- is in ae-tér-num, qui-a pí- us es. ℣. Ré- qui-em

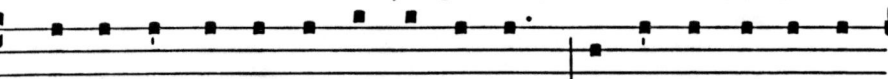

ae- tér-nam dó- na é - is, Dó- mi - ne, et lux per- pé- tu- a

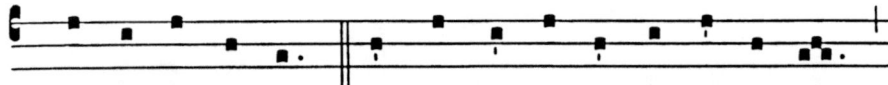

lú- ce- at é - is. * Cum sán- ctis tú - is in ae- tér- num,

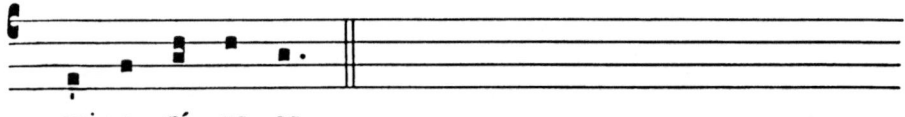

qui- a pí - us es.

Absolution after Mass

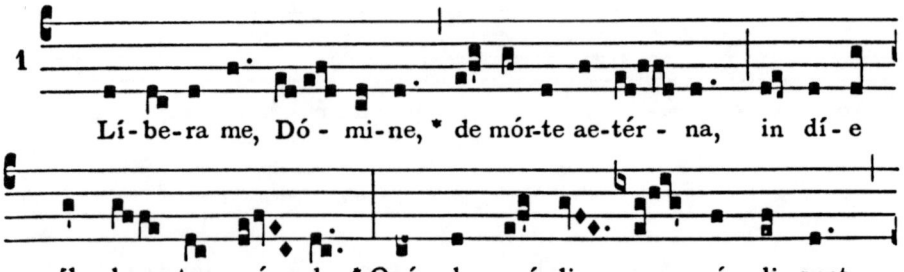

Lí- be-ra me, Dó- mi-ne, * de mór-te ae-tér - na, in dí - e

íl - la tre- mén- da: * Quán-do caé- li mo - vén-di sunt

dó-na é-is Dó-mi-ne: et lux per-pé-tu-a lú-ce-at é-is.

Repeat *Libera me* to ℣.

Rorate Caeli

[*This is the Introit [1] for the fourth Sunday of Advent.*]

Drop down dew, ye heavens, from above,
And let the clouds rain the just One;
Let the earth open,
And bud forth a Saviour.

The heavens tell the glory of God,
And the Firmament declareth the works of His hands.

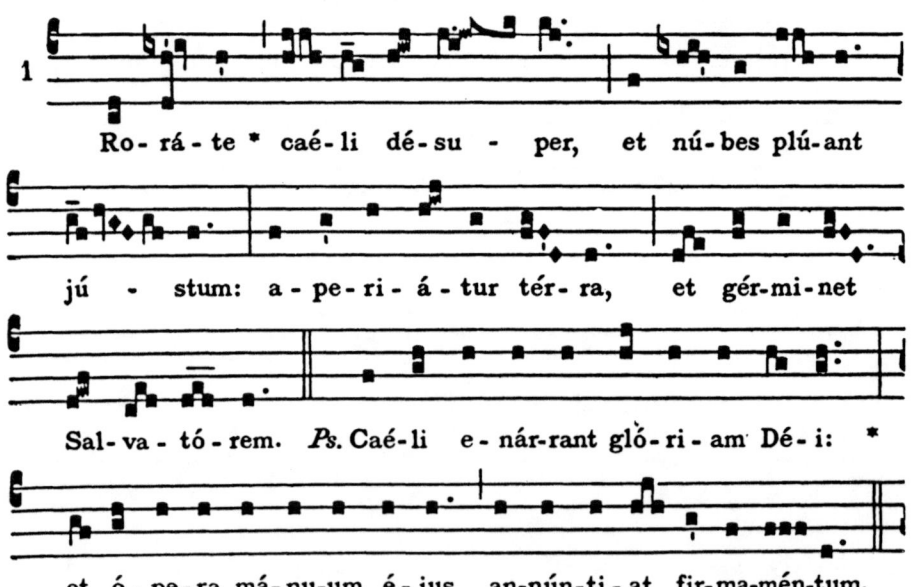

[1] The word *Introit* comes from the Latin word *introire*, meaning "to enter." The Introit in the Mass is the entrance chant. It is sung by the choir as the priest enters the sanctuary, and is afterwards read by the priest from the Epistle side of the altar.

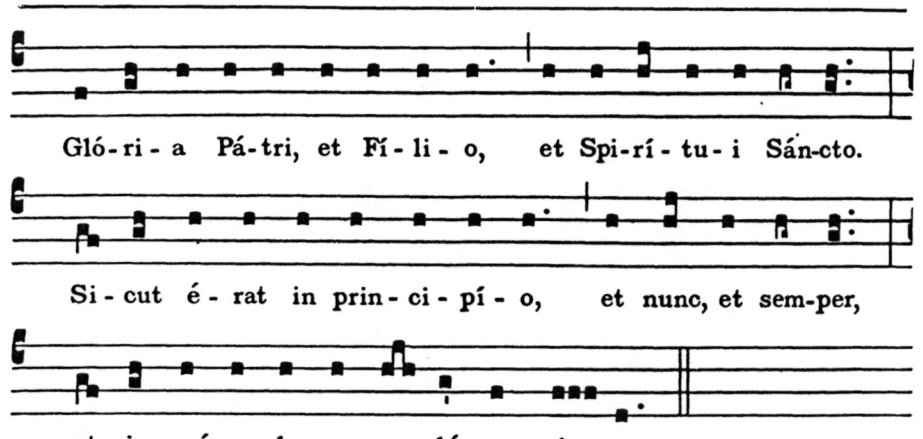

Gló-ri-a Pá-tri, et Fí-li-o, et Spi-rí-tu-i Sán-cto. Si-cut é-rat in prin-ci-pí-o, et nunc, et sem-per, et in saé-cu-la sae-cu-ló-rum. A-men.

Rorate Caeli

[*A hymn for Advent*]

Drop down dew, ye heavens, from above,
and let the clouds rain the just One.

Be not angry, Lord, and remember not
our iniquity forever. Lo! the city of
the Holy One is become a desert;
Jerusalem is a wilderness, our holy
and glorious house, where our fathers
praised Thee.

We have sinned, and we are all become
as one unclean, and we have all fallen
as a leaf. And our iniquities, like the
wind, have taken us away. Thou hast hidden
Thy face from us, and hast crushed us
in the hand of our iniquity.

See, Lord, the affliction of Thy people,
and send Him Whom Thou art to send.
Send forth the Lamb, the ruler of the earth,
from the rock of the desert to the mountain
of the daughter of Sion, that He Himself may
take from us the yoke of our captivity.

Be comforted, be comforted, my people.
Thy Salvation will come quickly.
Why dost thou waste away in sadness because
  grief hath again taken possession of thee?
I shall save thee. Fear not, for I am the
Lord thy God, the Holy One of Israel, thy Redeemer.

1. Ro-rá-te caé-li dé-su-per, et nú-bes plú-ant jus-tum. (*Repeat after each stanza*)

1. Ne i-ra-scá-ris Dó-mi-ne, ne ul-tra me-mí-ne-ris in-i-qui-tá-tis: ec-ce cí-vi-tas Sán-cti fá-cta est de-sér-ta: Sí-on de-sér-ta fá-cta est: Je-rú-sa-lem de-so-lá-ta est: dó-mus san-cti-fi-ca-ti-ó-nis tú-ae et gló-ri-ae tú-ae, u-bi lau-da-vé-runt te pá-tres nó-stri ℞. *Roráte.*

2. Pec-cá-vi-mus, et fá-cti sú-mus tam-quam im-mún-dus

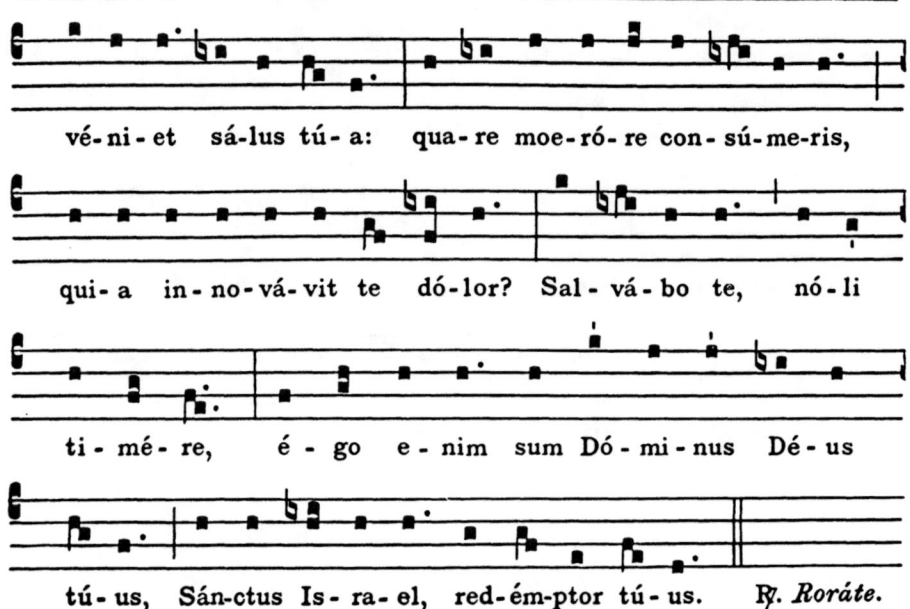

vé-ni-et sá-lus tú-a: qua-re moe-ró-re con-sú-me-ris, qui-a in-no-vá-vit te dó-lor? Sal-vá-bo te, nó-li ti-mé-re, é-go e-nim sum Dó-mi-nus Dé-us tú-us, Sán-ctus Is-ra-el, red-ém-ptor tú-us. ℟. Roráte.

Puer Natus in Bethlehem

[A Christmas hymn, written in the fourteenth century]

1. A child is born in Bethlehem, alleluia,
   Whence Jerusalem rejoices, alleluia, alleluia.

   Chorus
   In our heart's jubilation
   Let us adore with a new song Christ Who is born.

2. Here He lies in a manger, alleluia,
   Who is King eternally, alleluia, alleluia.

3. The ox and the ass know, alleluia,
   That this Child is the Lord; alleluia, alleluia.

4. And the Angel reveals to the shepherds, alleluia,
   That He is the Lord, alleluia, alleluia.

5. Kings come from Saba, alleluia.
   They offer gold, frankincense, and myrrh, alleluia, alleluia.

6. In this birthday joy, alleluia,
   Let us bless the Lord, alleluia, alleluia.

7. Praise be to the Holy Trinity, alleluia,
   Give thanks to God, alleluia, alleluia.

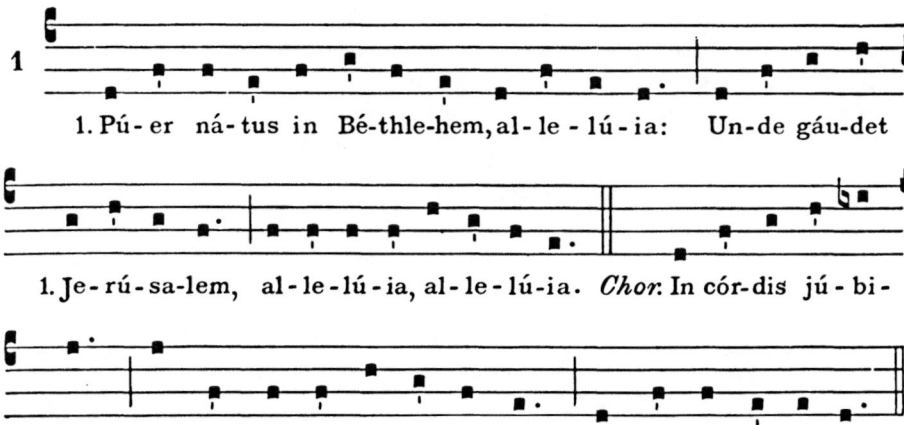

1. Pú-er ná-tus in Bé-thle-hem, al-le-lú-ia: Un-de gáu-det
1. Je-rú-sa-lem, al-le-lú-ia, al-le-lú-ia. *Chor.* In cór-dis jú-bi-lo Chrí-stum ná-tum a-do-ré-mus, Cum nó-vo cán-ti-co.

2. Hic jácet in praesépio, alleluia,
   Qui régnat sine término, alleluia, alleluia. *Chor.* In cordis.

3. Cognovit bos et asinus, alleluia,
   Quod puer erat Dominus, alleluia, alleluia. *Chor.* In cordis.

4. Et Angelus pastóribus, alleluia,
   Revélat quod sit Dominus, alleluia, alleluia. *Chor.* In cordis.

5. Reges de Saba véniunt, alleluia,
   Aurum, thus, mýrrham ófferunt, alleluia, alleluia. *Chor.* In cordis.

6. In hoc natáli gáudio, alleluia,
   Benedicamus Domino, alleluia, alleluia. *Chor.* In cordis.

7. Laudétur sáncta Trínitas, alleluia,
   Deo dicámus gratias, alleluia, alleluia. *Chor.* In cordis.

Puer Nobis Nascitur

A Child is born to us	They sing in joy to the Lord:
Who is also the Ruler of the Angels;	Glory in the highest,
He suffers in this world,	And to men of good heart
The Lord of lords.	Peace and salvation on earth.
The Angels announce to the shepherds	Let us at a time of such joy
That in Bethlehem	Sing to the Lord a song of jubilation,
He who was promised to men	And to the Son Who is born
Is now born, the Savior.	Let us offer loving hearts.

May He Who is born
Today of Mary
Lead us by His grace
To the eternal kingdom.

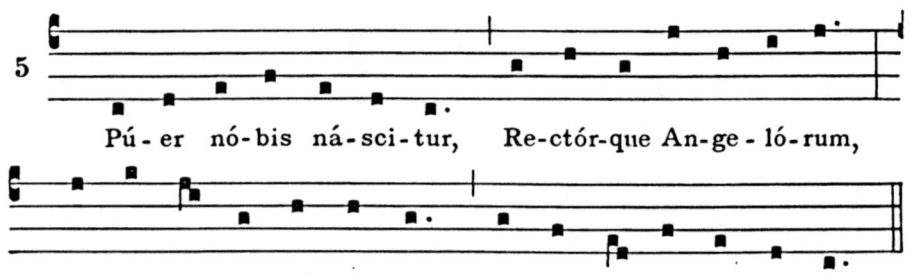

Pú-er nó-bis ná-sci-tur, Re-ctór-que An-ge-ló-rum,

In hoc mún-do pá-ti-tur, Dó-mi-nus do-mi-nó-rum.

Angeli pastóribus	Nos de táli gáudio
Núntiant, in Béthlehem	Dómino jubilémus,
Promíssum homínibus	Nascentíque Fílio
Nátum jam salvatórem.	Pia córda litémus.
Cánunt laéti Dómino	Qui nátus ex María
Glória in excélsis	In díe hodiérna
Hómini córde bóno	Perdúcat nos grátia
Pax et sálus in térris.	Ad régna sempitérna.

Dominus Dixit ad Me

[An anthem for the Nativity]

The Lord said to me: Thou art My Son, Today I have begotten Thee.

ANTIPHON[1]

Hodie Christus

Today Christ is born;
Today the Savior hath appeared;
Today Angels sing on earth,
And Archangels rejoice;
Today the just exult, saying:
Glory to God in the highest, alleluia.

[1] Antiphon or Anthem is a verse from Holy Scripture sung or recited before and after each psalm in parts of the Divine Office, and also before the Benedictus and Magnificat.

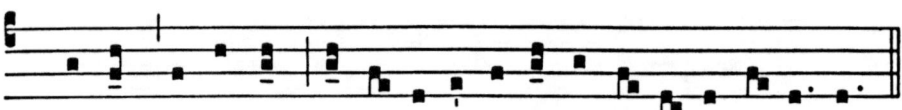

jú-sti, di-cén-tes: Gló-ri-a in ex-cél-sis Dé-o, al-le-lú-ia.

Quem Vidistis

[*For Christmas*]

Whom did you see, shepherds? Say.
Tell us who is He that has appeared on earth. (*They say*)
We have seen the newly born
And the celestial choirs singing in praise of the Lord, alleluia, alleluia.

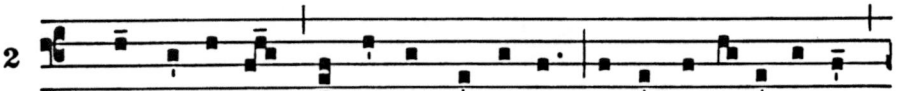

2 Quem vi-dí-stis,* pas-tó-res? dí-ci-te: an-nun-ti-á-te nó-bis,

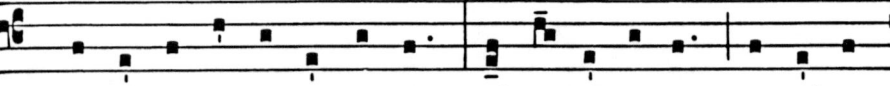

in tér-ris quis ap-pá-ru-it? Ná-tum ví-di-mus, et chó-ros

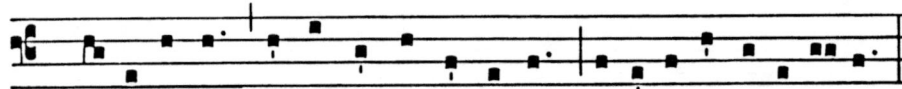

An-ge-ló-rum col-lau-dán-tes Dó-mi-num, al-le-lú-ia, al-le-lú-ia.

O Admirabile Commercium

[*An anthem for the season of Christmas*]

O wonderful exchange!
The Creator of the human race
Assuming our nature,
Deigned to be born of a Virgin,
   and coming forth, a Man without human generation,
Gave us to share His Divinity.

6 O ad-mi-rá-bi-le com-mér-ci-um! * Cre-á-tor

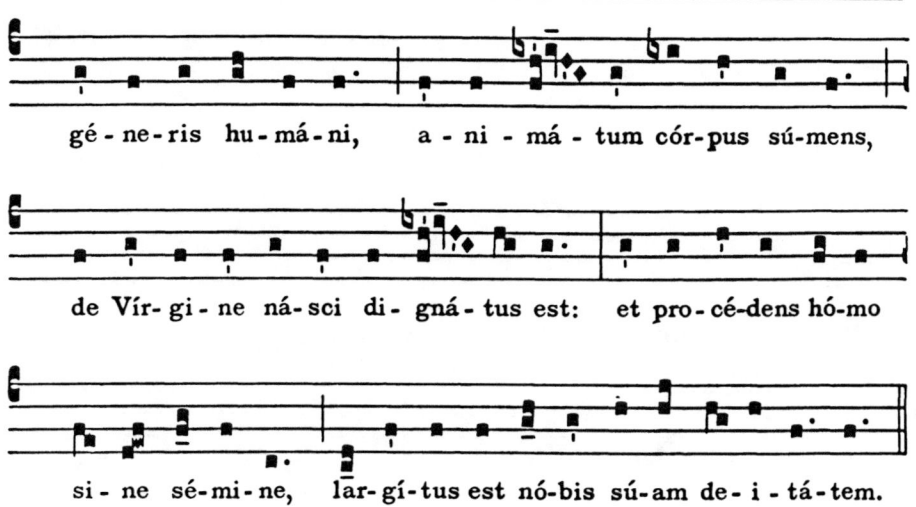

Attende Domine

[*A hymn for the season of Lent*]

Hearken, Lord, and have mercy, because we have sinned against Thee.
To Thee, sovereign King, Redeemer of mankind, we lift eyes filled with tears.

Hear, O Christ, and answer the prayers of Thy supplicants.

Right Hand of the Father, Cornerstone, Way of salvation,
Gate of Heaven, wash the stains of our guilt.

We beseech Thee, God of majesty, lend Thine ear to our groanings,
Graciously pardon our sins.

We confess to Thee the sins that we have committed.
With contrite heart we acknowledge our hidden sins.
May Thy love, O Redeemer, pardon us.

Thou, made captive though innocent, and led without resistance,
    was condemned by false witnesses in behalf of the impious.
Do Thou, Christ, keep those whom Thou hast redeemed.

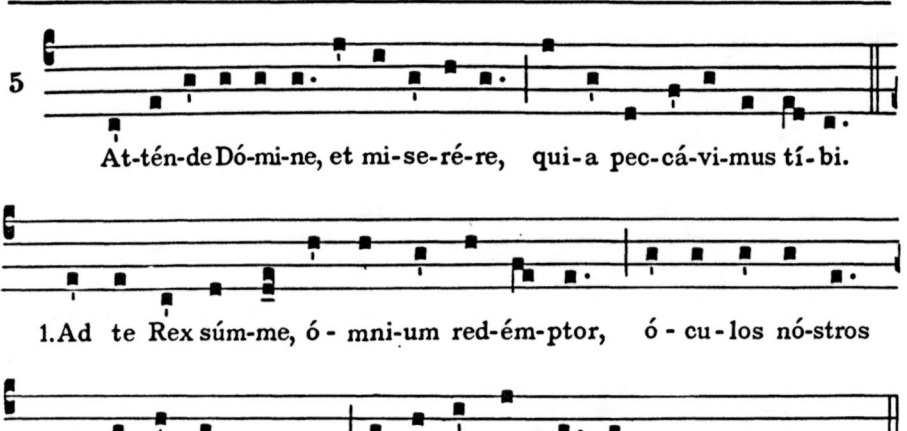

Attén-de Dómine, et mi-se-ré-re, qui-a pec-cá-vi-mus tí-bi.

1. Ad te Rex súm-me, ó-mni-um red-ém-ptor, ó-cu-los nó-stros sub-le-vá-mus flén-tes: ex-aú-di, Chrí-ste, sup-pli-cán-tum pré-ces.

Repeat *Attende* after each stanza.

2
Dextera Pátris, lápis anguláris,
vía salútis, jánua caeléstis
áblue nóstri máculas delícti.

3
Rogámus, Déus, tuam majestátem:
áuribus sácris gémitus exáudi:
crímina nóstra plácidus indúlge.

4
Tibi fatémur crimina admíssa:
contríto córde pándimus occúlta:
túa, Redémptor, píetas ignóscat.

5
Innocens cáptus, nec repúgnans dúctus,
téstibus fálsis pro ímpiis damnátus:
quos redemísti, tu consérva, Chríste.

Stabat Mater

[The Sequence for the Feast of the Seven Dolors of the Blessed Virgin Mary, Thirteenth Century.]

The sorrowful Mother stood,
Weeping, beside the cross
On which her Son hung.
Her anguished soul,
Grief-stricken and sorrowful,
A sword pierced.

Oh, how sad and afflicted
Was that blessed Mother
Of the sole-begotten One!
She grieved and sorrowed,
As a loving Mother, while she beheld
The pangs of her glorious Son.

Who would not weep To see Christ's mother In such anguish? Who would not but grieve with her On beholding Christ's Mother Sorrowing with her Son?	Ah! Mother, font of love, Make me feel the force of thy sorrow That I may mourn with thee. Make my heart burn With love for Christ, my God, That I with thee may please Him.
For the sins of His people, She saw Jesus in torment And condemned to the scourger. She saw her sweet Son Dying, forsaken As he gave up His spirit.	Holy Mother, grant me this: Fix the wounds of the Crucified Firmly in my heart. Of thy wounded Son Who deigned so to suffer for me Share with me the pangs.

Make me weep lovingly with thee,
Grieve with thee for the Crucified,
As long as I live.
To stand beside the cross with thee,
And to join in thy lamentation,
Is my desire.

Virgin of virgins, all-excelling,
Be not now bitter toward me.
Make me lament with thee.
Make me bear about the death of Christ,
A sharer of His passion be,
And let me ever contemplate His wounds.

Stá-bat Má-ter do-lo-ró-sa Jux-ta crú-cem la-cri-mó-sa, Dum pen-dé-bat Fí-li-us.

2. Cújus ánimam geméntem,
   Contristátam et doléntem
   Pertransívit gladius.

3. O quam trístis et afflícta
   Fuit ílla benedícta
   Máter unigéniti!

4. Quae maerébat et dolébat,
   Pia Máter, dum vidébat
   Náti poénas ínclyti.

5. Quis est hómo qui non fléret,
   Mátrem Chrísti se vidéret
   In tánto supplicío?

6. Quis non pósset contristári,
   Chrísti mátrem contemplári
   Doléntem cum Fílio?

7. Pro peccátis suae géntis,
   Vídit Jésum in torméntis,
   Et flagéllis súbditum.

8. Vídit súum dúlcem nátum
   Moriéndo desolátum,
   Dum emísit spíritum.

9. Eia Máter, fons amóris,
   Me sentíre vim dolóris
   Fac, ut técum lúgeam.

10. Fac ut árdeat cor méum
    In amándo Chrístum Déum,
    Ut síbi compláceam.

11. Sáncta Máter, ístud ágas,
    Crucifíxi fíge plágas
    Córdi méo válide.

12. Túi náti vulneráti,
    Tam dignáti pro me páti,
    Poénas mécum dívide.

13. Fac me técum pie flére,
    Crucifíxo condolére,
    Donec égo víxero.

14. Juxta crúcem técum stáre,
    Et me tíbi sociáre
    In plánctu desídero.

15. Vírgo vírginum praeclára,
    Míhi jam non sis amára:
    Fac me técum plángere.

Pueri Hebraeorum

[An antiphon which may be sung during the distribution of palms]

The children of the Hebrews, carrying olive branches, came to meet our Lord, crying out and saying: Hosanna in the highest!

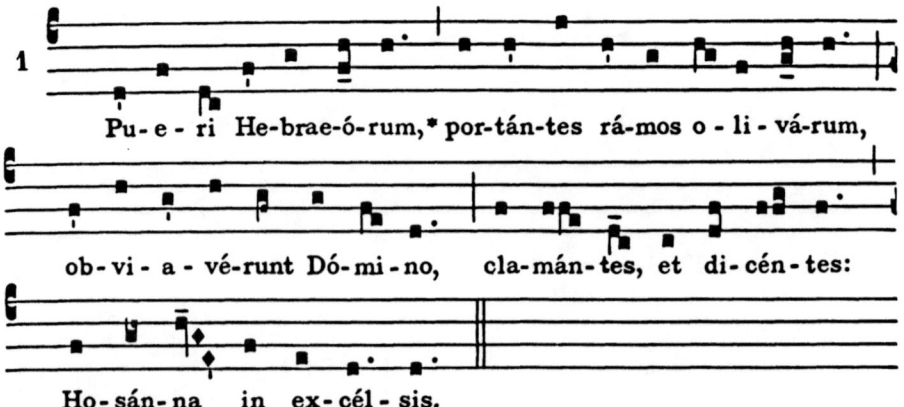

Pueri Hebraeorum

[Sung during the distribution of Palms]

The children of the Hebrews spread their garments in the way, and cried out, saying: Hosanna to the son of David; blessed is He who cometh in the name of the Lord:

Pu-e-ri He-brae-ó-rum * ve-sti-mén-ta pro-ster-né-bant in ví-a, et cla-má-bant di-cén-tes: Ho-sán-na fí-li-o Dá-vid: be-ne-dí-ctus qui vé-nit in nó-mi-ne Dó-mi-ni.

Gloria, Laus, et Honor

[A processional hymn for Palm Sunday. Ninth century]

Glory, praise, and honor be to Thee,
O Christ, Redeemer, King,
To Whom the flower of youth sang a loving Hosanna.

Thou art the King of Israel and David's noble Son,
O blessed King, Who comest in the name of the Lord.

The whole heavenly host praises Thee on high,
And mortal men and all created things together praise Thee.

The Hebrew people came to meet Thee with palms.
Lo! with prayers, vows, and hymns we present ourselves before Thee.

They were offering their homage of praise to Thee before Thy Passion;
Lo! we raise our song to Thee now reigning.

They were pleasing to Thee; may our devotion, too, please Thee,
Good King, gentle King,
To Whom all that is good is pleasing.

Crucem Tuam Adoramus

[*This is sung during the adoration of the Cross on Good Friday.*]

We adore Thy Cross, O Lord, and we praise and glorify Thy holy resurrection. For lo! by this wood joy came into the whole world. May God have mercy on us and bless us; may His countenance shine upon us, and may He have mercy on us.

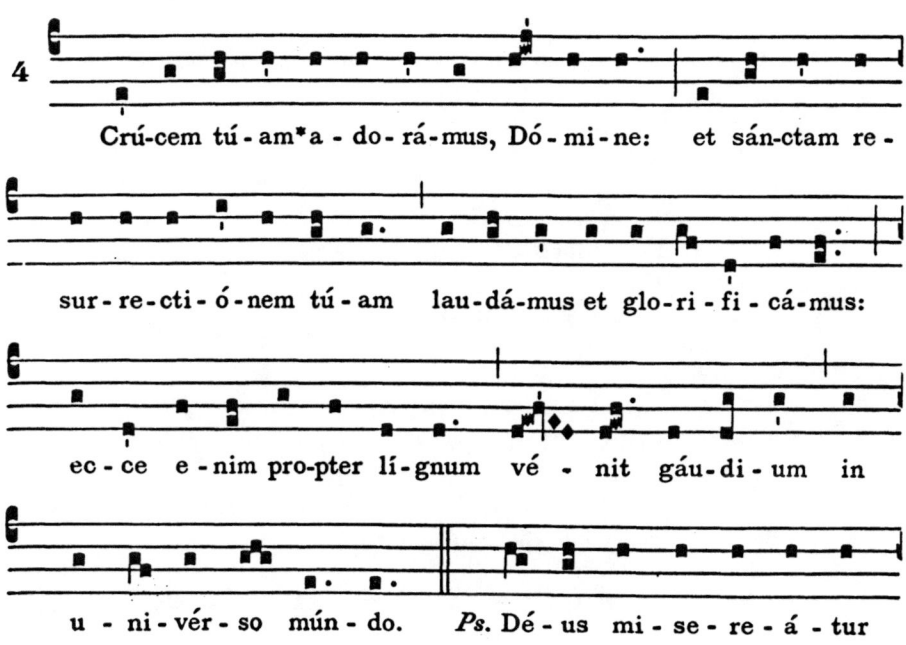

Repeat from the beginning to the *

Vexilla Regis

[*A processional hymn for Good Friday. Sixth century.*]

The standard of the King goes forth,
The mystic splendor of the Cross shines out,
The Cross on which Life suffered death,
And by death obtained life for us.

He, true Life, was wounded by the spear's cruel point,
And from that pierced side,
To wash away the defilement of our sins,
A stream of blood and water flowed.

Now is fulfilled what David
In truthful song foretold,
Saying to the world:
"God hath reigned by the Wood."

O glorious and shining Tree,
Adorned with the purple of the King,
Chosen, worthy with thy trunk
To touch such holy Limbs.

Blessed Tree, from whose arms
The world's ransom hung!
Thou, on whose beam was weighed this Sacred Body,
Didst rob hell of its prey.

Hail, Cross, sole hope of man,
Hail, at this Passion-tide!
Bestow increase of grace on loving hearts,
And blot out the sins of the guilty.

Thee, Trinity, fount of salvation,
Let all hearts unite to praise!
O Thou, Who givest victory through the Cross,
Grant also the reward.

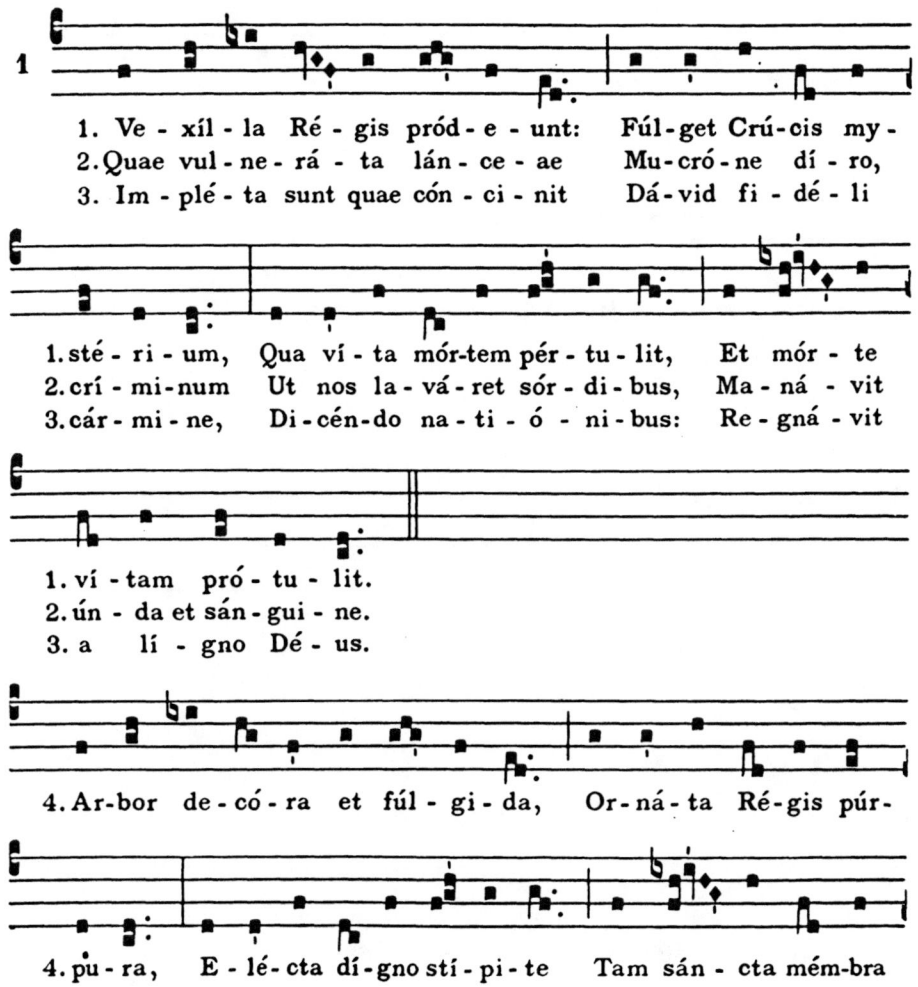

1. Ve - xíl - la Ré - gis pród - e - unt: Fúl - get Crú - cis my - sté - ri - um, Qua ví - ta mór - tem pér - tu - lit, Et mór - te ví - tam pró - tu - lit.
2. Quae vul - ne - rá - ta lán - ce - ae Mu - cró - ne dí - ro, Ut nos la - vá - ret sór - di - bus, Ma - ná - vit ún - da et sán - gui - ne.
3. Im - plé - ta sunt quae cón - ci - nit Dá - vid fi - dé - li cár - mi - ne, Di - cén - do na - ti - ó - ni - bus: Re - gná - vit a lí - gno Dé - us.
4. Ar - bor de - có - ra et fúl - gi - da, Or - ná - ta Ré - gis púr - pu - ra, E - lé - cta dí - gno stí - pi - te Tam sán - cta mém - bra

O Vos Omnes

[*An antiphon, or anthem, for Holy Saturday*]

O all you who pass by the way
Stop and see if there is any sorrow
Like unto My sorrow.

O vos ó-mnes,* qui trans-í-tis per ví-am, at-tén-di-te,
et vi-dé-te si est dó-lor sic-ut dó-lor mé-us.

Vespere

[*An antiphon for Holy Saturday*]

On the evening of the sabbath,
When it began to dawn toward the first day of the week,
Mary Magdalene and the other Mary
Came to see the sepulcher, alleluia.

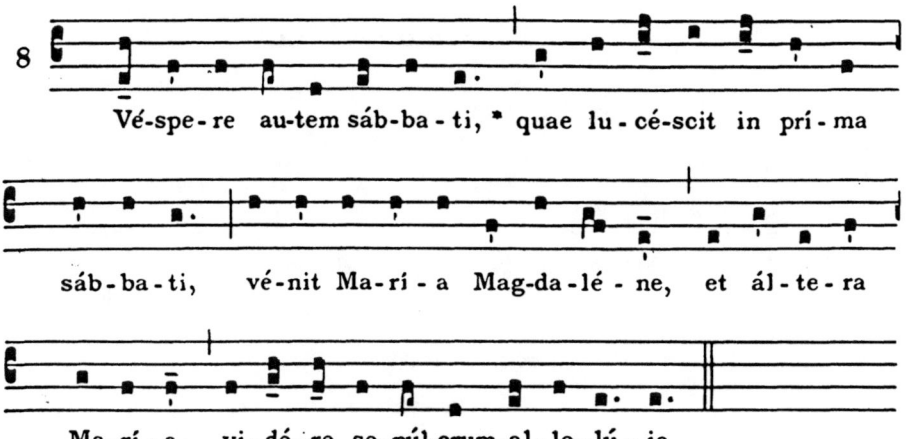

Vé-spe-re au-tem sáb-ba-ti, * quae lu-cé-scit in prí-ma
sáb-ba-ti, vé-nit Ma-rí-a Mag-da-lé-ne, et ál-te-ra
Ma-rí-a, vi-dé-re se-púl-crum, al-le-lú-ia.

Pascha Nostrum

[*Communion hymn for Easter*]

Christ our Pasch is sacrificed, alleluia,
Therefore, let us feast on the unleavened bread
Of sincerity and truth, alleluia, alleluia, alleluia.

Surrexit Dominus Vere

[*For Easter Sunday*]

The Lord hath truly risen, alleluia

Regina Caeli

[*Antiphon for Easter Sunday. Tenth century.*]

O Queen of Heaven rejoice, alleluia,
Because He whom thou wast found worthy to bear, alleluia,
Has risen as He said, alleluia,
Pray for us to God, alleluia.

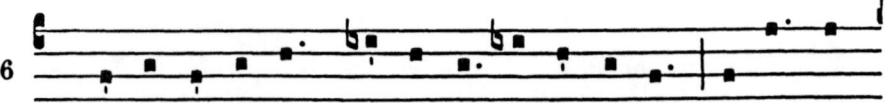

REPERTORY

me-ru-ís-ti por-tá-re, al-le-lú-ia: Re-sur-ré-xit, sí-cut dí-xit, al-le-lú-ia: O-ra pro nó-bis Dé-um, al-le-lú-ia.

Viri Galilaei

[*Antiphon from Second Vespers of the Ascension of our Lord*]

Men of Galilee,
Why are you looking up to heaven?
This Jesus, who was taken up from you into heaven,
Will come again, alleluia.

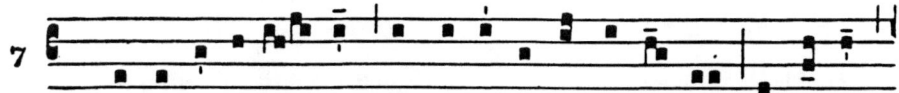

7 Ví-ri Ga-li-laé-i, * quid a-spí-ci-tis in caé-lum? Hic Jé-sus,

qui as-súm-ptus est a vó-bis in caé-lum, sic vé-ni-et, al-le-lú-ia.

Repleti Sunt

[*Antiphon for Pentecost*]

They were all filled
With the Holy Spirit,
And began to speak, alleluia

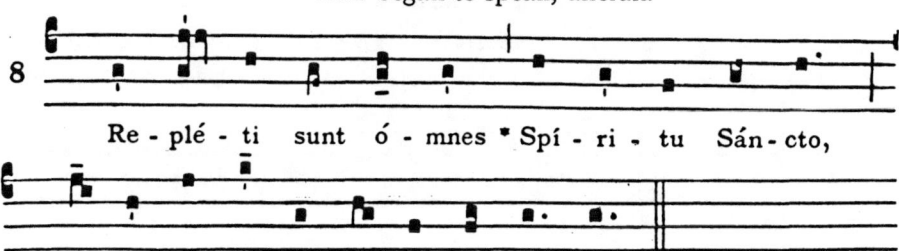

8 Re-plé-ti sunt ó-mnes * Spí-ri-tu Sán-cto, et coe-pé-runt ló-qui, al-le-lú-ia.

Veni Sancte Spiritus

[*Sequence for the Feast of Pentecost. Twelfth century*]

Come, Holy Spirit,	Without Thy divine power
And send from heaven	There is nothing in man,
A ray of Thy light.	Nothing that is guiltless.
Come, Father of the poor,	Wash what is defiled,
Come, Giver of gifts,	Water what is arid,
Come, Light of hearts;	Heal what is wounded,
Supreme Consoler,	Bend that which is rigid,
Sweet Guest of the soul,	Warm that which is cold,
Sweet Refreshment;	Put straight souls that have gone astray.
In labor, Rest,	Give to Thy faithful,
In heat, Coolness,	Who trust in Thee,
In tears, Consolation.	Thy seven sacred gifts.
O most blessed Light,	Give us the merit of virtue;
Fill the inmost recesses of the hearts	Give us a happy death;
of Thy faithful.	Give us eternal joy.

1. Vé-ni Sán-cte Spí-ri-tus, Et e-mít-te caé-li-tus Lú-cis tú-ae
2. Vé-ni pá-ter páu-per-um, Vé-ni dá-tor mú-ne-rum, Vé-ni lú-men

1. rá - di-um. 3. Con-so-lá-tor óp-ti-me, Dúl-cis hó-spes á-ni-mae, Dúl-ce
2. cór - di-um. 4. In la-bó-re ré-qui-es, In aés-tu tem-pé-ri-es, In flé-

3. re-fri-gé-ri-um. 5. O lux be-a-tís-si-ma, Ré-ple cór-dis ín-ti-ma
4. tu so-lá-ti-um. 6. Si-ne tú-o nú-mi-ne, Ni-hil est in hó-mi-ne,

5. Tu-ó-rum fi-dé-li-um. 7. Lá-va quod est sór-di-dum, Rí-ga quod est
6. Ni-hil est in-nó-xi-um. 8. Flé-cte quod est rí-gi-dum, Fó-ve quod est

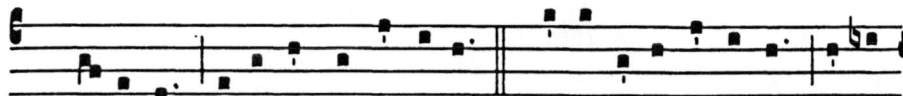

7. á-ri-dum, Sá-na quod est sáu-ci-um. 9. Da tú-is fi-dé-li-bus, In te
8. frí-gi-dum, Ré-ge quod est dé-vi-um. 10. Da vir-tú-tis mé-ri-tum, Da sa-

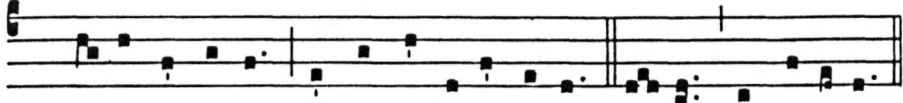

9. con-fi-dén-ti-bus, Sá-crum sep-te-ná-ri-um.   Al-le-lú-ia.
10. lú-tis éx-i-tum, Da per-én-ne gáu-di-um. A-men.

Veni Creator

[*Hymn for Pentecost. Ninth century*]

Come, Creator Spirit,
Visit the souls of Thy faithful,
Fill with heavenly grace
The hearts which Thou didst create.

Thou, Who art called the Paraclete,
Gift of the most high God,
Fountain of life, fire, love,
And spiritual unction.

Thou, sevenfold in Thy gift,
Finger of the right Hand of the Father,
Thou, the true promise of the Father,
Who dost enrich tongues with speech.

Enkindle light in our minds,
Pour love into our hearts,
Strengthen our weak flesh,
By Thy unfailing power.

Drive the enemy far from us,
And give us peace without delay.
With Thee as our guide,
May we avoid all harm!

Through Thee may it be given us
To know the Father and the Son;
And may we eternally believe in Thee,
Who art the Spirit of Them Both.

Glory be to God the Father,
And to the Son who rose
From the dead, and to the Paraclete,
World without end. Amen.

Ve-ni Cre-á-tor Spí-ri-tus, Mén-tes tu-ó-rum ví-si-ta:
Im-ple su-pér-na grá-ti-a Quae tu cre-á-sti pé-cto-ra.

2. Qui dí-ce-ris Pa-rá-cli-tus, Al-tís-si-mi dó-num Dé-i,
Fons ví-vus, í-gnis, cá-ri-tas, Et spi-ri-tá-lis ún-cti-o.

3. Tu se-pti-fór-mis mú-ne-re, Dí-gi-tus pa-tér-nae déx-te-rae,
Tu ri-te pro-mís-sum Pá-tris, Ser-mó-ne dí-tans gút-tu-ra.

O Sacrum Convivium

O sacred banquet in which Christ is received, the memory of His Passion is recalled, the soul is filled with grace, and the pledge of future glory is given us.

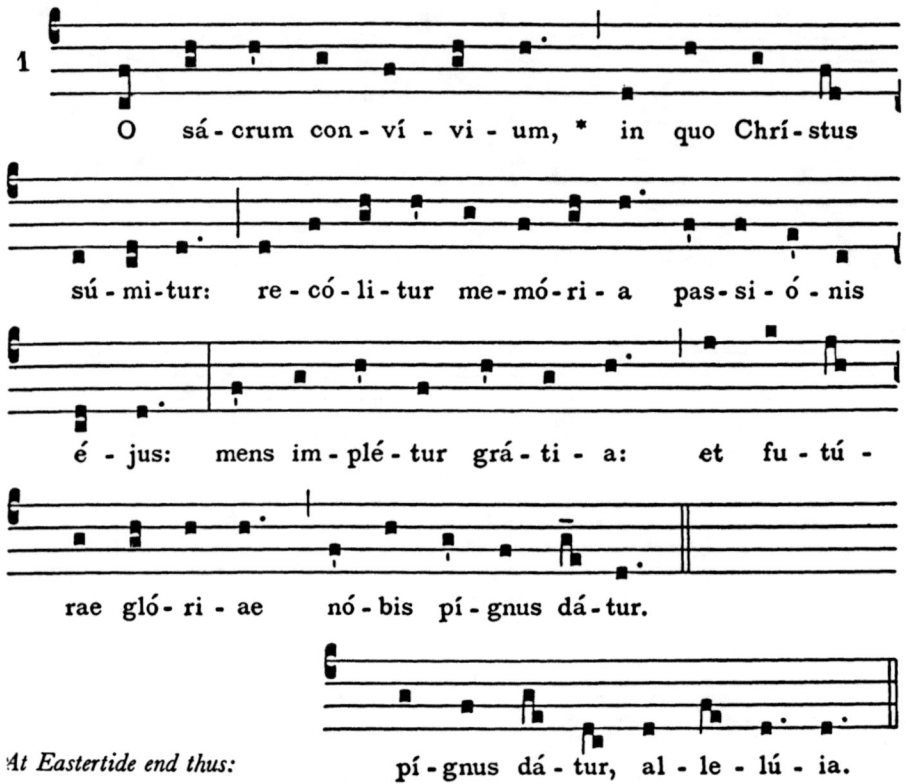

1. O sá-crum con-ví-vi-um, * in quo Chrí-stus sú-mi-tur: re-có-li-tur me-mó-ri-a pas-si-ó-nis é-jus: mens im-plé-tur grá-ti-a: et fu-tú-rae gló-ri-ae nó-bis pí-gnus dá-tur.

At Eastertide end thus: pí-gnus dá-tur, al-le-lú-ia.

Adoro Te

[*A Hymn to the Most Blessed Sacrament, written by St. Thomas Aquinas*]

I adore Thee devoutly, hidden God,
Who art truly hidden beneath these forms,
To Thee my heart submits itself entirely,
Because in contemplating Thee, it finds itself wholly helpless.

Sight, touch, and taste are deceived in Thee;
Hearing alone is safely believed.
I believe all that the Son of God hath said;
Nothing is truer than this Word of Truth.

On the cross only God was hidden,
But here Manhood too is hid,
Yet, I, believing both and confessing both,
Beg that for which the penitent thief begged.

Though I do not gaze upon Thy wounds, as Thomas did,
Yet, I acknowledge Thee to be my God.
Make me ever more and more believe in Thee,
Have hope in Thee, and love Thee.

O reminder of my Lord's dying,
Living Bread that givest life to man,
Grant that my soul may find its life in Thee,
And ever savor Thy sweetness.

Loving Pelican, Jesus Lord,
Cleanse me unclean in Thy Blood,
A single drop of which can save
The entire world from all its sin.

Jesus, whom I now see veiled,
Grant, I pray, that for which I so thirst,
May I, beholding Thee face to face unveiled,
Be happy in the vision of Thy glory.

5. 1. A - dó - ro te, de - vó - te, la - tens Dé - i - tas, Quae sub his fi - gú - ris vé - re lá - ti - tas: Tí - bi se cor mé - um

tó-tum súb-ji-cit, Qui-a, te con-tém-plans, tó-tum dé-fi-cit.

A - men.

To be sung at the close of the hymn.

2. Visus, tactus, gustus in te fállitur,
   Sed audítu solo tuto créditur:
   Credo quidquid dixit Dei Fílius,
   Nil hoc verbo veritátis vérius.

3. In cruce latébat sola Déitas,
   At hic latet simul et humánitas;
   Ambo tamen credens atque cónfitens,
   Peto quod petívit latro páenitens.

4. Plagas, sicut Thomas, non intúeor,
   Deum tamen meum te confíteor:
   Fac me tibi semper magis crédere,
   In te spem habére, te dilígere.

5. O memoriále mortis Domini,
   Panis vivus, vitam praestans hómini,
   Praesta meae menti de te vivere,
   Et te illi semper dulce sápere.

6. Pie pellicáne, Jesu Dómine
   Me immundum munda tuo sanguine,
   Cujus una stilla salvum fácere
   Totum mundum quit ab omni scélere.

7. Jesu, quem velátum nunc aspício,
   Oro fiat illud quod tam sítio:
   Ut te reveláta cernens fácie,
   Visu sim beátus tuae glóriae. Amen.

Ecce Panis Angelorum

[*The following hymn consists of the four last stanzas of the* Lauda Sion, *which is the Sequence for Corpus Christi. This Sequence was written by* St. Thomas Aquinas.]

Lo! the Bread of Angels
Is made the food of pilgrims;
Truly Bread of the children of God,
And not to be cast to dogs.

It was foretold by ancient types:
The sacrifice of Isaac,
The offering of the Paschal lamb,
The manna given to our fathers.

Good Shepherd, true Bread,
Jesus, have mercy on us!
Feed us, protect us,
Make us to see good things
In the land of the living.

Thou Who dost know and canst do all things,
Thou Who dost feed us in our mortal life on earth,
Make us Thy guests at Thy Banquet in heaven,
Fellow-heirs and companions of
Heaven's citizens, the saints.

Ec-ce pá-nis An-ge-ló-rum, Fá-ctus cí-bus vi-a-tó-rum: Vé-re pá-nis fi-li-ó-rum, Non mit-tén-dus cá-ni-bus. In fi-gú-ris prae-si-gná-tur, Cum I-sa-ac im-mo-lá-tur, A-gnus Pá-schae

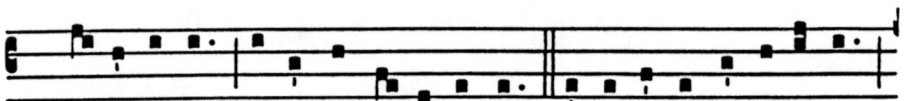
de-pu-tá-tur, Dá-tur mán-na pá-tri-bus. Bó-ne Pá-stor, pá-nis vé-re,

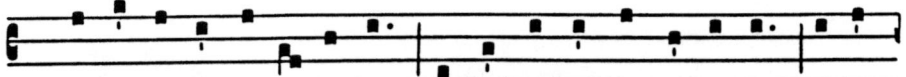
Jé-su, nó-stri mi-se-ré-re: Tu nos pá-sce, nos tu-é-re, Tu nos

bó-na fac vi-dé-re In tér-ra vi-vén-ti-um. Tu qui cún-cta scis et

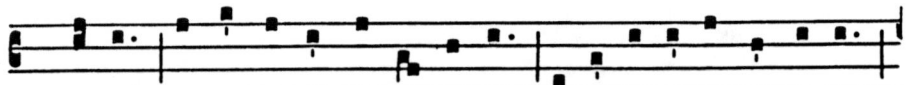
vá-les, Qui nos pá-scis hic mor-tá-les: Tú-os i-bi com-men-sá-les,

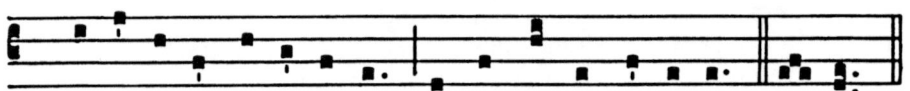
Co-he-ré-des et so-dá-les Fac san-ctó-rum cí-vi-um. A-men.

Pange Lingua

[*Hymn to the Most Blessed Sacrament, written by* ST. THOMAS AQUINAS]

Sing, my tongue, the mystery
  Of the glorious Body,
And of the Precious Blood,
Shed for the world's redemption
By the King of the gentiles,
Fruit of a noble womb.

Given to us, He was born for us
  Of a spotless Virgin;
And, having lived in the world,

And sown the seed of His word,
He brought to a close His sojourn here
With a wonderful institution.

On the night of the Last Supper,
While at table with His brethren,
When He had fully observed the law
In the ordained feast,
He gave Himself with His own hands
As Food to His band of twelve.

The Word-made-Flesh, by His word,
Makes His Flesh to be true Bread;
And wine becomes the Blood of Christ.
If the intellect fails to understand,
Faith alone suffices
To strengthen the sincere heart.

Therefore, before this great Sacrament,
Let us bend low in adoration!
Let the Old Law
Give way to the New Rite.
Let faith supply
Where the senses fail!

To the Father and the Son
Praise and song of joy,
Together with salvation, honor,
Power, and blessing!
And to Him Who proceeds from Both
Equal be the praise!

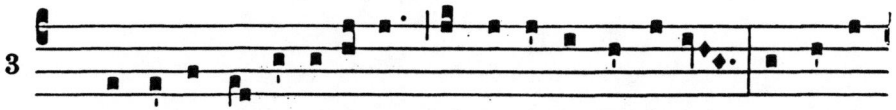
Pan-ge lín-gua glo-ri-ó-si Cór-po-ris my-sté-ri-um, San-gui-nís-

que pre-ti-ó-si, Quem in mún-di pré-ti-um Frú-ctus vén-tris

ge-ne-ró-si Rex ef-fú-dit gén-ti-um. A-men.

Nóbis dátus, nóbis nátus
Ex intácta Vírgine,
Et in múndo conversátus,
Spárso vérbi sémine,
Sui móras incolátus
Míro cláusit órdine.

Vérbum cáro, pánem vérum
Vérbo cárnem éfficit:
Fítque sánguis Chrísti mérum,
Et si sénsus déficit,
Ad firmándum cor sincérum
Sóla fídes súfficit.

In supréme nocte coenae
Recumbens cum frátribus,
Observáta lége pléne
Cíbis in legálibus,
Cíbum turbae duodénac
Se dat súis mánibus.

Tántum ergo Sacraméntum
Venerémur cérnui:
Et antíquum documéntum
Nóvo cédat rítui:
Praéstet fídes suppleméntum
Sénsuum deféctui.

Genitóri, Genitóque
Laus et jubilátio,
Sálus, hónor, vírtus quoque
Sit et benedíctio:
Procedénti ab utróque
Cómpar sit laudátio. Amen.

O Salutaris Hostia

[*A hymn to the Most Blessed Sacrament, written by* St. Thomas Aquinas]

O saving Victim,
Who dost open the gate of heaven,
Wars with our enemies press upon us.
Give strength, bring help.

To the one and triune Lord,
Let eternal praise be given;
And may He grant us life without end
In our true native land. Amen.

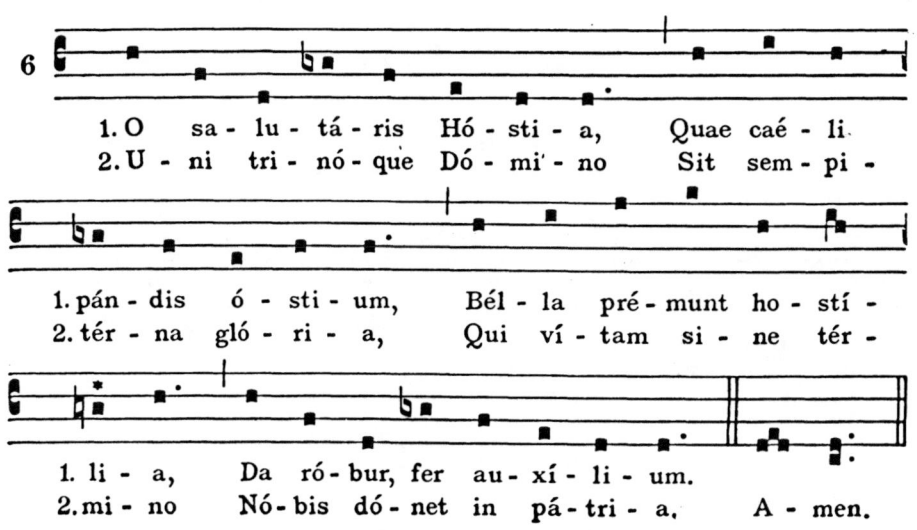

O Salutaris

1. O sa - lu - tá - ris Hó - sti - a, Quae caé - li pán - dis ó -
2. U - ni tri - nó - que Dó - mi - no Sit sem - pi - tér - na gló -

* The cancel sign in Gregorian notation is made just like the same sign in modern notation.

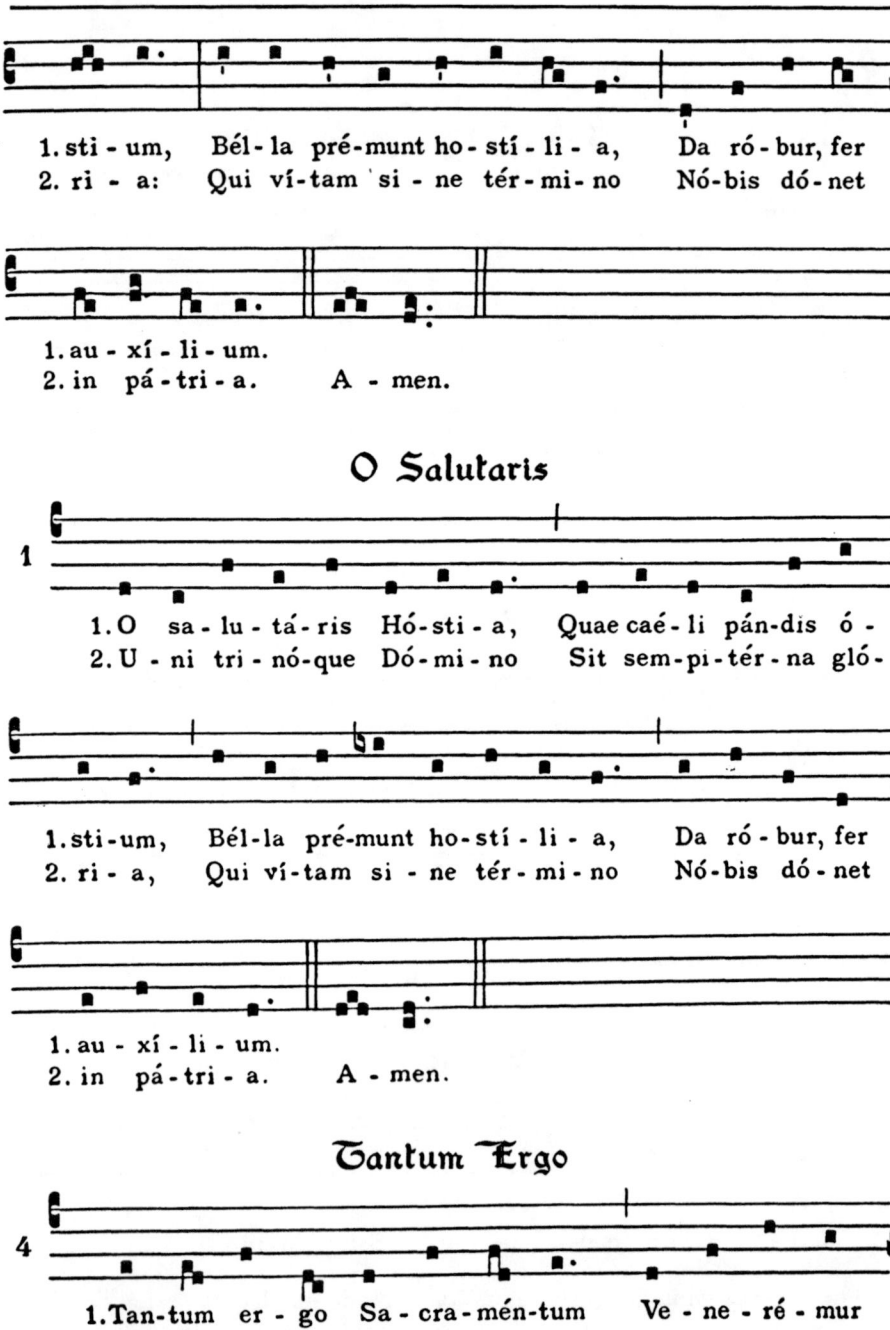

REPERTORY

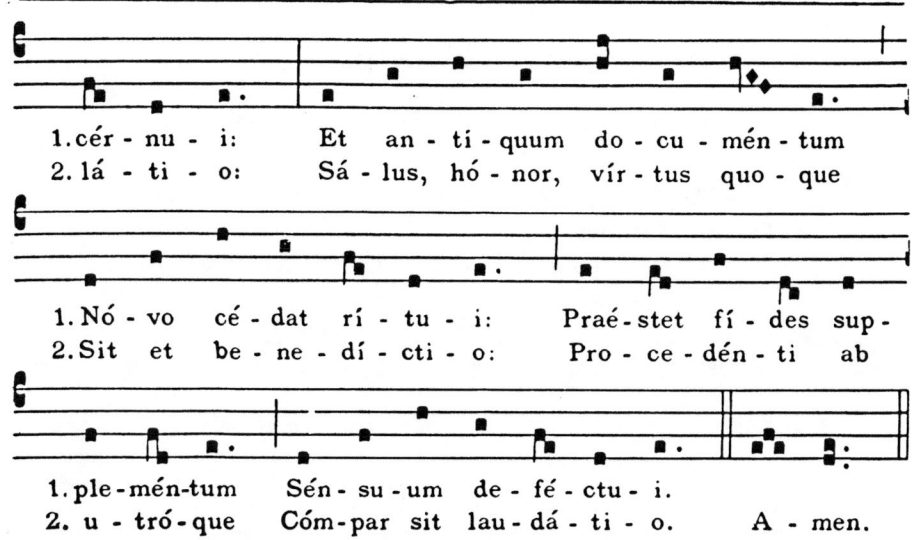

Salva Nos

[*An Evening Anthem*]

Save us, O Lord, when we watch,
Guard us when we sleep,
So that we may watch with Christ,
And rest in peace. Alleluia.

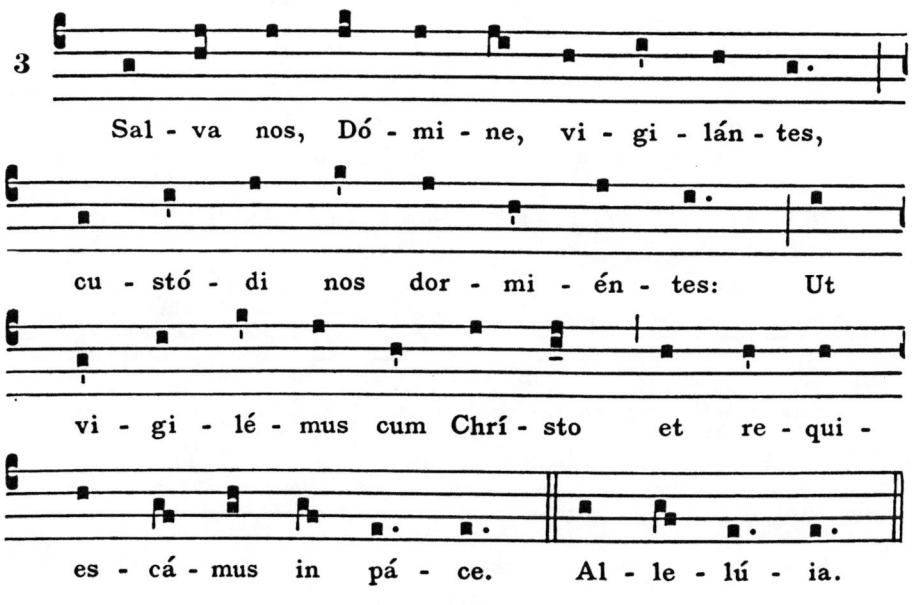

Sancti Angeli

[*A vesper antiphon for the Feast of the Guardian Angels, October 2*]

Holy Angels, our Guardians,
Defend us in battle,
That we may not perish in the dreadful judgment.

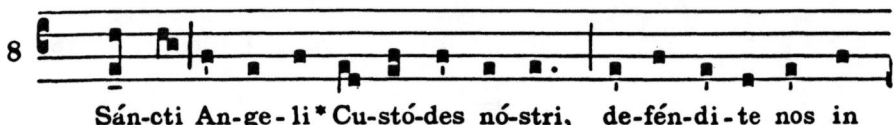

Sán-cti An-ge-li * Cu-stó-des nó-stri, de-fén-di-te nos in

praé-li-o, ut non per-e-á-mus in tre-mén-do ju-dí-ci-o.

Beati Mundo

[*Communion hymn for the Feast of All Saints, November 1*]

Blessed are the clean of heart,
For they shall see God.

Blessed are the peacemakers,
For they shall be called the children of God.

Blessed are they who suffer persecution for justice's sake,
For theirs is the Kingdom of Heaven.

Be-á-ti mún-do cór-de, * quó-ni-am í-psi Dé-um
vi-dé-bunt: be-á-ti pa-cí-fi-ci: quó-ni-am fí-li-i

O Quam Gloriosum Est Regnum

[*Antiphon for the Feast of All Saints, November 1*]

O how beautiful is the kingdom
   Wherein Christ
Reigns amid His Saints.
Clothed in white garments,
They follow the Lamb
Whithersoever He goeth.

Creator Alme Siderum

[*Vesper hymn for Advent*]

Bountiful Creator of the skies,
Eternal light of those who believe in Thee,
Jesus, Redeemer of all,
Heed the prayers of Thy suppliants.

Thee we entreat,
Great Judge of the last day,
By the weapons of heavenly grace,
Defend us from our enemies.

Power, honor, praise, and glory
To God the Father with the Son,
And likewise to the Holy Paraclete,
World without end.

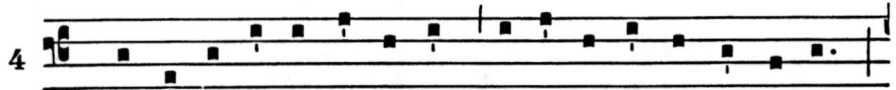

1. Cre-á-tor ál-me sí-de-rum, Ae-tér-na lux cre-dén-ti-um,

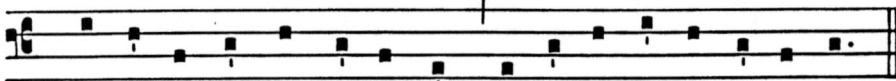

Jé-su, Red-ém-ptor ó-mni-um, In-tén-de vó-tis súp-pli-cum.

Te deprecamur, ultimae
Magnum diei Judicem,
Armis supernae gratiae
Defende nos ab hostibus.

Virtus, honor, laus, gloria
Deo Patri cum Filio,
Sancto simul Paraclito,
In saeculorum saecula.

Jesu Dulcis Memoria

[*A hymn in honor of the Most Holy Name of Jesus. Twelfth Century*]

Sweet is the thought of Jesus,
It gives true joys of the heart.
Above honey and all things
Is His sweet presence.

Nothing lovelier is sung,
Nothing more pleasant is heard,
Nothing sweeter is thought
Than Jesus, the Son of God.

O Jesus, hope of penitent souls,
How kind Thou art to those who ask of Thee,
How good to those who seek Thee!
But what art Thou not to those who find Thee?

No tongue can say,
No word express;
Only he who has experienced it
Can know what it is to love Jesus.

Jesus, be Thou our joy,
Who art to be our reward!
May we find our glory in Thee!
Through all eternity.

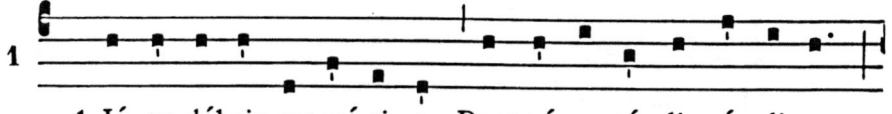

1. Jé-su dúl-cis me-mó-ri-a, Dans vé-ra cór-dis gáu-di-a:

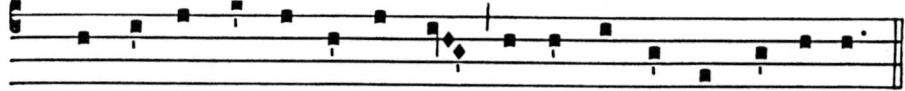

Sed su-per mel et ó-mni-a, E-jus dúl-cis prae-sén-ti-a.

2. Nil cánitur suávius,
   Nil audítur jucúndius,
   Nil cogitátur dulcius,
   Quam Jésus Déi Fílius.

3. Jesu spes paeniténtibus,
   Quam píus es peténtibus!
   Quam bónus te quaeréntibus!
   Sed quid inveniéntibus?

4. Nec língua válet dícere,
   Nec líttera exprímere:
   Expértus pótest crédere,
   Quid sit Jésum dilígere.

5. Sis Jésu nóstrum gáudium,
   Qui es futúrus praémium:
   Sit nóstra in te glória,
   Per cúncta semper sáecula

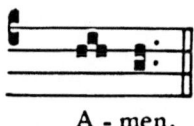

A - men.

Te Joseph Celebrent

Thee, Joseph, may the hosts of heaven praise,
May the choirs of Christians all together sing thy name,
Thou who, renowned for thy saintly life,
Wast joined in a chaste bond to the glorious Virgin.

Thou didst hold in thy embrace the new-born Lord,
And followed His flight to Egypt's distant shores.
Lost in Jerusalem, thou didst seek and find Him,
Thus mingling joy with tears.

Trinity, most high,
Spare us as we pray,
Grant that, through the merits of Joseph,
We may ascend to the starry realm,
And there at last raise unendingly to Thee our grateful song.

Te Jó-seph cé - le-brent á - gmi-na caé - li-tum: Te cún-cti

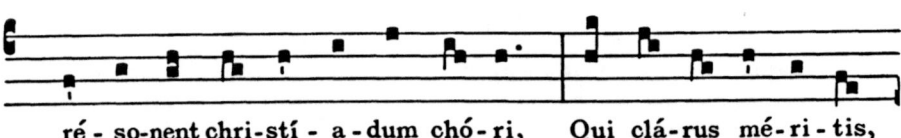

ré - so-nent chri-stí - a - dum chó - ri, Qui clá-rus mé-ri-tis,

jún-ctus es ín-cly-tae Cá-sto foé-de-re Vír-gi-ni.

Tu natum Dóminum stríngis, ad exteras
Aegýpti prófugum tu sequeris plagas:
Amíssum Solymis quaéris, et ínvenis,
Míscens gáudia flétibus.

Nóbis, súmma Trías, párce precántibus:
Da Joseph méritis sídera scándere:
Ut tandem líceat nos tibi perpetim
Grátum prómere cánticum.

Beata Mater

[*Antiphon for the Feast of the Most Holy Rosary*]

Blessed Mother and spotless Virgin,
Glorious Queen of the world,
Let all feel Thy helping power,
Who celebrate Thy feast of the most Holy Rosary.

Be-á-ta Má-ter * et in-tá-cta Vír-go, glo-ri-ó-sa

Re-gí-na mún-di, sén-ti-ant ó-mnes tú-um

ju-vá-men, qui-cúm-que cé-le-brant tú-am san-

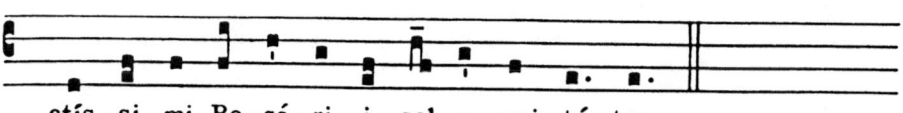
ctís-si-mi Ro-sá-ri-i sol-e-mni-tá-tem.

Alma Redemptoris

[Antiphon in honor of the Blessed Virgin Mary. It is sung from the first Sunday of Advent to the Feast of the Purification, February 2. Eleventh Century]

Sweet Mother of the Redeemer,
Thou that abidest Heaven's open gate,
And the Star of the Sea,
Help thy fallen people,
Who are trying to rise.
Thou, who, while nature marveled, didst bear
Thy Holy Creator, and didst remain a Virgin both before and after,
Receiving from Gabriel's lips that *Ave*,
Have mercy on sinners.

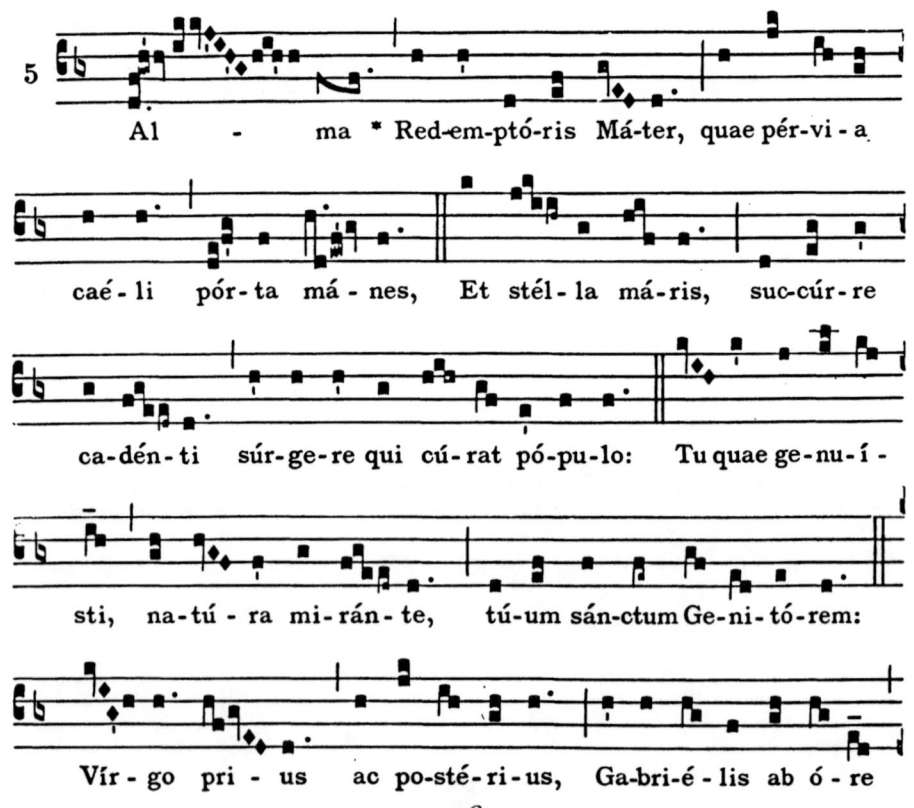

Al - ma * Red-em-ptó-ris Má-ter, quae pér-vi-a caé-li pór-ta má-nes, Et stél-la má-ris, suc-cúr-re ca-dén-ti súr-ge-re qui cú-rat pó-pu-lo: Tu quae ge-nu-í-sti, na-tú-ra mi-rán-te, tú-um sán-ctum Ge-ni-tó-rem: Vír-go pri-us ac po-sté-ri-us, Ga-bri-é-lis ab ó-re

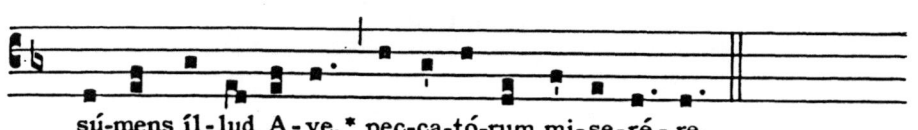

sú-mens íl-lud A-ve,* pec-ca-tó-rum mi-se-ré-re.

Ave Regina

Hail, Queen of the Heavens,
Hail, Mistress of the Angels,
Hail, Root of Jesse; Hail, Portal
Whence Light shone upon the world.

Rejoice, glorious Virgin,
Loveliest of all virgins,
Hail, O Thou exceeding fair,
Pray to Christ for us.

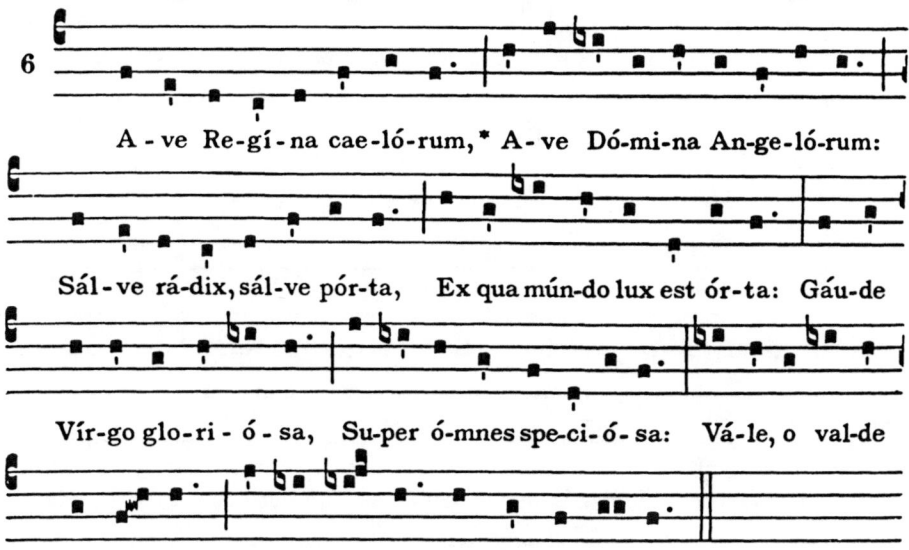

A-ve Re-gí-na cae-ló-rum,* A-ve Dó-mi-na An-ge-ló-rum:
Sál-ve rá-dix, sál-ve pór-ta, Ex qua mún-do lux est ór-ta: Gáu-de
Vír-go glo-ri-ó-sa, Su-per ó-mnes spe-ci-ó-sa: Vá-le, o val-de
de-có-ra, Et pro nó-bis Chrí-stum ex-ó-ra.

Salve Regina

[*Eleventh Century*]

Hail, Queen, Mother of mercy:
Our life, our sweetness and our hope, hail.
To thee we cry,
We exiles and sons of Eve.

To thee we sigh,
Groaning and weeping in this vale of tears.
Come then, our advocate,
Turn toward us those merciful eyes;

And show us after this exile
Jesus, the blessed fruit of thy womb.
O gentle, O kind,
O sweet Virgin Mary.

5. Sál-ve, Re-gí-na, *Má-ter mi-se-ri-cór-di-ae: Ví-ta, dul-cé-do, et spes nó-stra, sál-ve. Ad te cla-má-mus, éx-su-les, fí-li-i Hé-vae. Ad te sus-pi-rá-mus, ge-mén-tes et flén-tes in hac la-cri-má-rum vál-le. E-ia er-go, Ad-vo-cá-ta nó-stra, íl-los tú-os mi-se-ri-cór-des ó-cu-los ad nos con-vér-te. Et Jé-sum, be-ne-dí-ctum frú-ctum vén-tris tú-i, nó-bis post hoc ex-sí-li-um o-stén-de. O clé-mens, O pí-a, O dúl-cis Vír-go Ma-rí-a.

Ave Maris Stella

Hail, Star of the sea,
Sweet Mother of God,
Ever a Virgin,
Happy Gate of Heaven!

Receiving that *Ave*
From the lips of Gabriel,
Establish us in peace,
Reversing the name Eva.

Loose the bonds of sinners,
Bring light to the blind,
Drive away our evils,
Ask for all good things.

Show that thou art a Mother.
Through thee may He receive our prayers
Who, when born for us,
Deigned to be thy Son.

Virgin all-excelling,
Meekest of mankind,
Free us from our sins,
Make us meek and chaste.

Keep our life pure,
Make safe our journey,
That, seeing Jesus,
We may rejoice forever with thee.

Praise to God the Father,
Glory to Christ the King,
And to the Holy Spirit!
To the Three be equal honor!

1. A - ve má - ris stél-la, Dé-i Má-ter ál - ma, At-que sem-per Vír-go, Fé-lix caé-li pór-ta. A - men. *(after last stanza)*

2. Súmens íllud Ave
   Gabriélis óre,
   Fúnda nos in páce,
   Mútans Hévae nómen.

3. Sólve víncla réis,
   Prófer lúmen caécis,
   Mála nóstra pélle,
   Bóna cúncta pósce.

4. Mónstra te ésse mátrem:
   Súmat per te préces,
   Qui pro nóbis nátus,
   Túlit ésse túus.

5. Vírgo singuláris,
   Inter ómnes mítis,
   Nos cúlpis solútos
   Mítes fac et cástos.

*The extra note will be needed on *te*, fourth stanza.

6. Vítam praésta púram,
   Iter pára tútum,
   Ut vidéntes Jésum
   Semper collaetémur.

7. Sit laus Déo Pátri,
   Summo Chrísto décus,
   Spirítui Sáncto,
   Tríbus hónor únus. Amen.

Salve Mater

Hail, mother of mercy,
Mother of God, mother of pardon,
Mother of hope, mother of grace,
Mother, full of holy joy,
O Mary!

Hail, glory of the human race,
Hail, Virgin above all virgins esteemed,
Who dost surpass all virgins,
And art enthroned above them in heaven,
O Mary!

Hail, happy Virgin and mother,
For He Who sitteth at the right hand of the Father,
Ruling heaven, earth, and air,
Took up His abode in Thy womb,
O Mary!

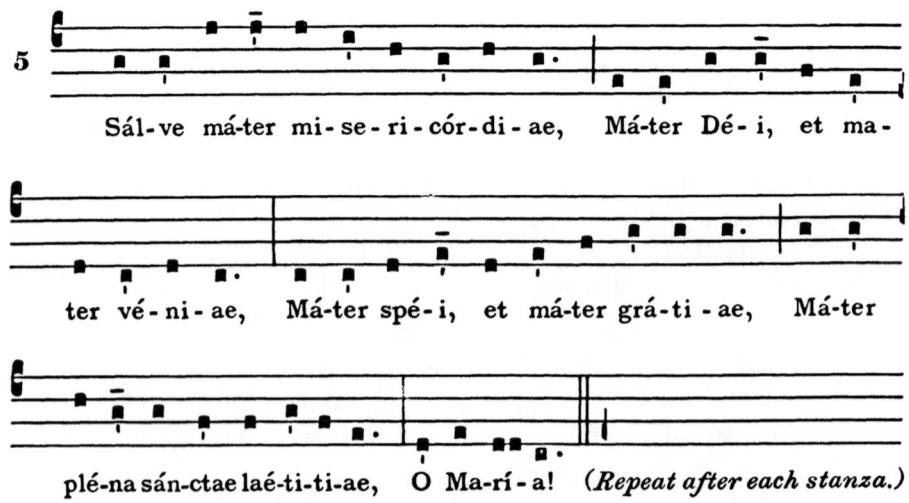

Sál-ve má-ter mi-se-ri-cór-di-ae, Má-ter Dé-i, et ma-ter vé-ni-ae, Má-ter spé-i, et má-ter grá-ti-ae, Má-ter plé-na sán-ctae laé-ti-ti-ae, O Ma-rí-a! *(Repeat after each stanza.)*

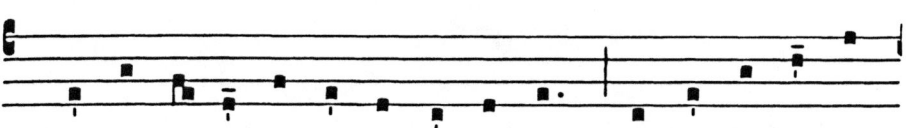

1. Sál-ve dé-cus hu-má-ni gé-ne-ris, Sál-ve Vir-go di-
2. Sál-ve fé-lix Vír-go pu-ér-pe-ra: Nam qui sé-det in

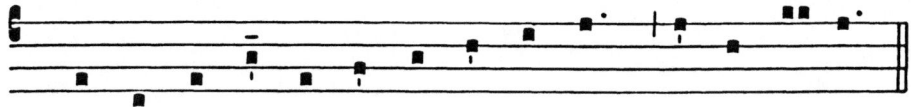

1. gní-or cé-te-ris, Quae vír-gi-nes ó-mnes trans-gré-de-ris,
2. Pa-tris dé-xte-ra, Caé-lum ré-gens, tér-ram et aé-the-ra,

1. Et ál-ti-us sé-des in sú-pe-ris, O Ma-rí-a!
2. In-tra tú-a se cláu-sit vís-ce-ra, O Ma-rí-a!

Index

Adoro te devote	110	Ictus	10
Alma redemptoris	126		
Ambrosian Gloria	73	Jesu dulcis memoria	122
Asperges	37		
Attende Domine	93	Kinds of Chant	12
Ave Maria	37		
Ave maris stella	129	Liquescent neums	19
Ave Regina Caelorum	127		
Ave Verum	29	Masses	
		I. Lux et origo	41
Beata Mater	125	II. Kyrie fons bonitatis	44
Beati Mundo	120	VIII. De Angelis	47
Bistropha	20		
Breath marks	11	IX. Cum jubilo	51
		X. Alme Pater	55
Consonants	14	XI. Orbis factor	58
Clefs	6	XVII. Mass for Sundays of Advent and Lent	61
Climacus	16		
Climacus resupinus	17	Mass for the Dead	75
Clivis	15		
Creator alme siderum	122	Modes	9
Credo I	63		
Credo III	66	Neums	15
Crucem tuam	99	Notation	7
Dies irae	76	O admirabile commercium	92
Diphthongs	14	O filii et filiae	32
Dominants	9	O quam gloriosum	121
Dominus dixit ad me	90	O sacrum convivium	110
		O Salutaris Hostia	116, 117, 118
Ecce Panis Angelorum	113	O vos omnes	102
Ecclesiastical pronunciation of Latin	14	Pacificus	31
Episema	19	Pange lingua	114
		Panis Angelicus	30
Finals	9	Pascha nostrum	103
Gloria, laus et honor	97	Pes subpunctis	18
Gloria Patri — mode IV	27	Pes subpunctis resupinus	18
Gregorian scales	9	Podatus	15
Guide	12	Porrectus	16
		Porrectus flexus	19
Hodie Christus natus est	91	Pressus	20

Presentation of modes	21	Salve Mater	130
Mode I	22	Salve Regina	127
Mode II	25	Sancti Angeli	120
Mode III	26	Scandicus	16
Mode IV	27	Scandicus flexus	17
Mode V	28	Scandicus subpunctis	18
Mode VI	28	Singing of Chant	11
Mode VII	30	Stabat Mater	94
Mode VIII	31	Staff (The)	6
		Story of Gregorian Chant	3
Puer natus in Bethlehem	88	Surrexit Dominus vere	104
Puer nobis nascitur	90	Syllables	8
Pueri Hebraeorum portantes	96		
Pueri Hebraeorum vestimenta	97	Tantum ergo	25, 26, 28, 118
		Te Joseph celebrent	124
Quem vidistis	92	Tonics	9
Quilisma	20	Torculus	16
		Torculus resupinus	17
		Torculus resupinus flexus	18
Regina caeli	104	Transposition	31
Repleti sunt	105	Tristropha	20
Responses	69		
Rhythm	10	Veni Creator	107
Rorate caeli (introit)	84	Veni Sancte Spiritus	106
Rorate caeli (hymn)	85	Vespere autem sabbati	103
		Vexilla Regis	100
Salicus	16	Victimae paschali	23
Salicus flexus	17	Vidi aquam	39
Salva nos Domine	119	Viri Galilaei	105

Printed in the United States
107415LV00004B/145/A